# WAYS of WORLDMAKING

Other Books by Nelson Goodman

# NELSON GOODMAN

# WAYS of WORLDMAKING

HACKETT PUBLISHING COMPANY

The first four chapters have been separately published as follows:

"Words, Works, Worlds" in *Erkenntnis*, volume 9, 1975;
"The Status of Style" in *Critical Inquiry*, volume 1, 1975;
"Some Questions Concerning Quotation" in *The Monist*, volume 58, 1974;
"When Is Art?" in *The Arts and Cognition*, The Johns Hopkins University Press, 1977.

The cooperation of the several editors and publishers is gratefully acknowledged.

Copyright © 1978 by Nelson Goodman

Printed in the United States of America

Fifth Printing, 1988

Library of Congress Catalog Card Number 78-56364
ISBN 0–915144–52–2

For further information, please address
Hackett Publishing Company, Inc., Box 44937,
Indianapolis, Indiana 46204

*For K. S. G.,*

who makes worlds with watercolors

# CONTENTS

# FOREWORD

This book does not run a straight course from beginning to end. It hunts; and in the hunting, it sometimes worries the same raccoon in different trees, or different raccoons in the same tree, or even what turns out to be no raccoon in any tree. It finds itself balking more than once at the same barrier and taking off on other trails. It drinks often from the same streams, and stumbles over some cruel country. And it counts not the kill but what is learned of the territory explored.

For the third time in my life, work on a book has been spurred by an invitation to give a series of lectures. Special Lectures at the University of London led to *Fact*, *Fiction*, *and Forecast*. John Locke Lectures at Oxford University became *Languages of Art*. And the first Immanuel Kant Lectures at Stanford University provided the impetus for the present book and the basis for its last four chapters, although most of the final chapter is new. The first chapter was read at the University of Hamburg on the one-hundredth anniversary of the birth of Ernst Cassirer; and the first four chapters have appeared as separate papers.

The list of those who have helped is, as usual, impossibly long and I can mention only Stanford University and its Philosophy Department, especially Patrick Suppes; my colleagues Israel Scheffler, W. V. Quine, and Hilary Putnam; and my Project Zero associates Paul Kolers and Vernon Howard.

Since the seven chapters have been written and rewritten during some seven years and are often variations upon recurrent themes rather than consecutive steps in an argument, repetitions are inevitable and I hope forgivable. My experience with students and commentators has not convinced me that reiteration is needless. Inconsistencies are less forgivable, and I trust fewer. Obvious inadequacies are for the convenience of critics.

Few familiar philosophical labels fit comfortably a book that is at odds with rationalism and empiricism alike, with materialism and idealism and dualism, with essentialism and existentialism, with mechanism and vitalism, with mysticism and scientism, and with most other ardent doctrines. What emerges can perhaps be described as a radical relativism under rigorous restraints, that eventuates in something akin to irrealism.

Nevertheless, I think of this book as belonging in that mainstream of modern philosophy that began when Kant exchanged the structure of the world for the structure of the mind, continued when C. I. Lewis exchanged the structure of the mind for the structure of concepts, and that now proceeds to exchange the structure of concepts for the structure of the several symbol systems of the sciences, philosophy, the arts, perception, and everyday discourse. The movement is from unique truth and a world fixed and found to a diversity of right and even conflicting versions or worlds in the making.

HARVARD UNIVERSITY

The following abbreviations are used throughout the book:

*SA*   for the third edition of *The Structure of Appearance*, D. Reidel Publishing Co., 1977 (first published 1951);

*FFF* for the third edition of *Fact, Fiction, and Forecast*, Hackett Publishing Co., 1977 (first published 1954);

*LA*   for the second edition of *Languages of Art*, Hackett Publishing Co., 1976 (first published 1968);

*PP*   for *Problems and Projects*, Hackett Publishing Company, 1972.

# I

# Words, Works, Worlds

## 1. Questions

Countless worlds made from nothing by use of symbols—so might a satirist summarize some major themes in the work of Ernst Cassirer. These themes—the multiplicity of worlds, the speciousness of 'the given', the creative power of the understanding, the variety and formative function of symbols—are also integral to my own thinking. Sometimes, though, I forget how eloquently they have been set forth by Cassirer,[1] partly perhaps because his emphasis on myth, his concern with the comparative study of cultures, and his talk of the human spirit have been mistakenly associated with current trends toward mystical obscurantism, anti-intellectual intuitionism, or anti-scientific humanism. Actually these attitudes are as alien to Cassirer as to my own skeptical, analytic, constructionalist orientation.

My aim in what follows is less to defend certain theses that Cassirer and I share than to take a hard look at some crucial questions they raise. In just what sense are there many worlds? What distinguishes genuine from spurious worlds? What are worlds made of? How are they made? What role do symbols play in the making? And how is worldmaking related to knowing? These questions must be faced even if full and final answers are far off.

---

[1] E.g. in *Language and Myth*, translated by Susanne Langer (Harper, 1946).

## 2. Versions and Visions

As intimated by William James's equivocal title *A Pluralistic Universe*, the issue between monism and pluralism tends to evaporate under analysis. If there is but one world, it embraces a multiplicity of contrasting aspects; if there are many worlds, the collection of them all is one. The one world may be taken as many, or the many worlds taken as one; whether one or many depends on the way of taking.[2]

Why, then, does Cassirer stress the multiplicity of worlds? In what important and often neglected sense are there many worlds? Let it be clear that the question here is not of the possible worlds that many of my contemporaries, especially those near Disneyland, are busy making and manipulating. We are not speaking in terms of multiple possible alternatives to a single actual world but of multiple actual worlds. How to interpret such terms as "real", "unreal", "fictive", and "possible" is a subsequent question.

Consider, to begin with, the statements "The sun always moves" and "The sun never moves" which, though equally true, are at odds with each other. Shall we say, then, that they describe different worlds, and indeed that there are as many different worlds as there are such mutually exclusive truths? Rather, we are inclined to regard the two strings of words not as complete statements with truth-values of their own but as elliptical for some such statements as "Under frame of reference *A*, the sun always moves" and "Under frame of reference *B*, the sun never moves"—statements that may both be true of the same world.

Frames of reference, though, seem to belong less to what is described than to systems of description: and each of the two statements relates what is described to such a system. If I ask

---

[2] But see further VII:1 below.

about the world, you can offer to tell me how it is under one or more frames of reference; but if I insist that you tell me how it is apart from all frames, what can you say? We are confined to ways of describing whatever is described. Our universe, so to speak, consists of these ways rather than of a world or of worlds.

The alternative descriptions of motion, all of them in much the same terms and routinely transformable into one another, provide only a minor and rather pallid example of diversity in accounts of the world. Much more striking is the vast variety of versions and visions in the several sciences, in the works of different painters and writers, and in our perceptions as informed by these, by circumstances, and by our own insights, interests, and past experiences. Even with all illusory or wrong or dubious versions dropped, the rest exhibit new dimensions of disparity. Here we have no neat set of frames of reference, no ready rules for transforming physics, biology, and psychology into one another, and no way at all of transforming any of these into Van Gogh's vision, or Van Gogh's into Canaletto's. Such of these versions as are depictions rather than descriptions have no truth-value in the literal sense, and cannot be combined by conjunction. The difference between juxtaposing and conjoining two statements has no evident analogue for two pictures or for a picture and a statement. The dramatically contrasting versions of the world can of course be relativized: each is right under a given system—for a given science, a given artist, or a given perceiver and situation. Here again we turn from describing or depicting 'the world' to talking of descriptions and depictions, but now without even the consolation of intertranslatability among or any evident organization of the several systems in question.

Yet doesn't a right version differ from a wrong one just in applying to the world, so that rightness itself depends upon and implies a world? We might better say that 'the world' depends upon rightness. We cannot test a version by comparing it with a world undescribed, undepicted, unperceived, but only by other means that I shall discuss later. While we may speak of determining what versions are right as 'learning about the world', 'the world' supposedly being that which all right versions describe, all we learn about the world is contained in right versions of it; and while the underlying world, bereft of these, need not be denied to those who love it, it is perhaps on the whole a world well lost. For some purposes, we may want to define a relation that will so sort versions into clusters that each cluster constitutes a world, and the members of the cluster are versions of that world; but for many purposes, right world-descriptions and world-depictions and world-perceptions, the ways-the-world-is, or just versions, can be treated as our worlds.[3]

Since the fact that there are many different world-versions is hardly debatable, and the question how many if any worlds-in-themselves there are is virtually empty, in what non-trivial sense are there, as Cassirer and like-minded pluralists insist, many worlds? Just this, I think:  that many different world-versions are of independent interest and importance, without any requirement or presumption of reducibility to a single base. The pluralist, far from being anti-scientific, accepts the sciences at full value.  His typical adversary is the monopolistic materialist or physicalist who maintains that one system, physics, is preeminent and all-inclusive, such that every other version must eventually be reduced to it or rejected as false or meaningless. If all right versions could somehow be reduced to one and only one, that one might with some semblance of

---

[3] Cf. "The Way the World Is" (1960), *PP*, pp. 24–32, and Richard Rorty, "The World Well Lost", *Journal of Philosophy*, Vol. 69 (1972), pp. 649–665.

plausibility[4] be regarded as the only truth about the only world. But the evidence for such reducibility is negligible, and even the claim is nebulous since physics itself is fragmentary and unstable and the kind and consequences of reduction envisaged are vague. (How do you go about reducing Constable's or James Joyce's world-view to physics?) I am the last person likely to underrate construction and reduction.[5] A reduction from one system to another can make a genuine contribution to understanding the interrelationships among world-versions; but reduction in any reasonably strict sense is rare, almost always partial, and seldom if ever unique. To demand full and sole reducibility to physics or any other one version is to forego nearly all other versions. The pluralists' acceptance of versions other than physics implies no relaxation of rigor but a recognition that standards different from yet no less exacting than those applied in science are appropriate for appraising what is conveyed in perceptual or pictorial or literary versions.

So long as contrasting right versions not all reducible to one are countenanced, unity is to be sought not in an ambivalent or neutral *something* beneath these versions but in an overall organization embracing them. Cassirer undertakes the search through a cross-cultural study of the development of myth, religion, language, art, and science. My approach is rather through an analytic study of types and functions of symbols and symbol systems. In neither case should a unique result be anticipated; universes of worlds as well as worlds themselves may be built in many ways.

---

[4] But not much, for no one type of reducibility serves all purposes.

[5] Cf. "The Revision of Philosophy" (1956), *PP*, pp. 5–23; and also *SA*.

### 3. How Firm a Foundation?

The non-Kantian theme of multiplicity of worlds is closely akin to the Kantian theme of the vacuity of the notion of pure content. The one denies us a unique world, the other the common stuff of which worlds are made. Together these theses defy our intuitive demand for something stolid underneath, and threaten to leave us uncontrolled, spinning out our own inconsequent fantasies.

The overwhelming case against perception without conception, the pure given, absolute immediacy, the innocent eye, substance as substratum, has been so fully and frequently set forth—by Berkeley, Kant, Cassirer, Gombrich,[6] Bruner,[7] and many others—as to need no restatement here. Talk of unstructured content or an unconceptualized given or a substratum without properties is self-defeating; for the talk imposes structure, conceptualizes, ascribes properties. Although conception without perception is merely *empty*, perception without conception is *blind* (totally inoperative). Predicates, pictures, other labels, schemata, survive want of application, but content vanishes without form. We can have words without a world but no world without words or other symbols.

The many stuffs—matter, energy, waves, phenomena—that worlds are made of are made along with the worlds. But made from what? Not from nothing, after all, but *from other worlds*. Worldmaking as we know it always starts from worlds already on hand; the making is a remaking. Anthropology and developmental psychology may study social and individual histories of

---

[6] In *Art and Illusion* (Pantheon Books, 1960), E. H. Gombrich argues in many passages against the notion of 'the innocent eye'.

[7] See the essays in Jerome S. Bruner's *Beyond the Information Given* [hereinafter *BI*], Jeremy M. Anglin, ed. (W. W. Norton, 1973). Chap. I.

such world-building, but the search for a universal or necessary beginning is best left to theology.[8] My interest here is rather with the processes involved in building a world out of others.

With false hope of a firm foundation gone, with the world displaced by worlds that are but versions, with substance dissolved into function, and with the given acknowledged as taken, we face the questions how worlds are made, tested, and known.

## 4. Ways of Worldmaking

Without presuming to instruct the gods or other worldmakers, or attempting any comprehensive or systematic survey, I want to illustrate and comment on some of the processes that go into worldmaking. Actually, I am concerned more with certain relationships among worlds than with how or whether particular worlds are made from others.

### (a) Composition and Decomposition

Much but by no means all worldmaking consists of taking apart and putting together, often conjointly: on the one hand, of dividing wholes into parts and partitioning kinds into subspecies, analyzing complexes into component features, drawing distinctions; on the other hand, of composing wholes and kinds out of parts and members and subclasses, combining features into complexes, and making connections. Such composition or decomposition is normally effected or assisted or consolidated by the application of labels: names, predicates, gestures, pic-

---

[8] Cf. *SA*, pp. 127–145; and "Sense and Certainty" (1952) and "The Epistemological Argument" (1967), *PP*, pp. 60–75. We might take construction of a history of successive development of worlds to involve application of something like a Kantian regulative principle, and the search for a first world thus to be as misguided as the search for a first moment of time.

tures, etc. Thus, for example, temporally diverse events are brought together under a proper name or identified as making up 'an object' or 'a person'; or snow is sundered into several materials under terms of the Eskimo vocabulary. Metaphorical transfer—for example, where taste predicates are applied to sounds—may effect a double reorganization, both re-sorting the new realm of application and relating it to the old one (*LA:* II).

Identification rests upon organization into entities and kinds. The response to the question "Same or not the same?" must always be "Same what?"[9] Different soandsos may be the same such-and-such: what we point to or indicate, verbally or otherwise, may be different events but the same object, different towns but the same state, different members but the same club or different clubs but the same members, different innings but the same ball game. 'The ball-in-play' of a single game may be comprised of temporal segments of a dozen or more baseballs. The psychologist asking the child to judge constancy when one vessel is emptied into another must be careful to consider *what* constancy is in question—constancy of volume or depth or shape or kind of material, etc.[10] Identity or constancy in a world is identity with respect to what is within that world as organized.

Motley entities cutting across each other in complicated patterns may belong to the same world. We do not make a new world every time we take things apart or put them together in another way; but worlds may *differ* in that not everything belonging to one belongs to the other. The world of the

---

[9] This does not, as sometimes is supposed, require any modification of the Leibniz formula for identity, but merely reminds us that the answer to a question "Is this the same as that?" may depend upon whether the "this" and the "that" in the question refer to thing or event or color or species, etc.

[10] See *BI*, pp. 331–340.

Eskimo who has not grasped the comprehensive concept of snow differs not only from the world of the Samoan but also from the world of the New Englander who has not grasped the Eskimo's distinctions.  In other cases, worlds differ in response to theoretical rather than practical needs.  A world with points as elements cannot be the Whiteheadian world having points as certain classes of nesting volumes or having points as certain pairs of intersecting lines or as certain triples of intersecting planes.  That the points of our everyday world can be equally well defined in any of these ways does not mean that a point can be identified in any one world with a nest of volumes and a pair of lines and a triple of planes; for all  these are different from each other.  Again the world of a system taking minimal concrete phenomena as atomic cannot admit qualities as atomic parts of these concreta.[11]

Repetition as well as identification is relative to organization. A world may be unmanageably heterogeneous or unbearably monotonous according to how events are sorted into kinds. Whether or not today's experiment repeats yesterday's, however much the two events may differ, depends upon whether they test a common hypothesis; as Sir George Thomson puts it:

There will always be something different.... What it comes to when you say you repeat an experiment is that you repeat all the features of an experiment which a theory determines are relevant. In other words you repeat the experiment as an example of the theory.[12]

Likewise, two musical performances that differ drastically are nevertheless performances of the same work if they conform to

[11] See further SA, pp. 3–22, 132–135, 142–145.

[12] In "Some Thoughts on Scientific Method" (1963), in *Boston Studies in the Philosophy of Science*, Vol. 2 (Humanities Press, 1965), p. 85.

the same score. The notational system distinguishes constitutive from contingent features, thus picking out the performance-kinds that count as works (*LA*, pp. 115–130). And things 'go on in the same way' or not according to what is regarded as the same way; 'now I can go on',[13] in Wittgenstein's sense, when I have found a familiar pattern, or a tolerable variation of one, that fits and goes beyond the cases given. Induction requires taking some classes to the exclusion of others as relevant kinds. Only so, for example, do our observations of emeralds exhibit any regularity and confirm that all emeralds are green rather than that all are grue (i.e. examined before a given date and green, or not so examined and blue—*FFF*, pp. 72–80). The uniformity of nature we marvel at or the unreliability we protest belongs to a world of our own making.

In these latter cases, worlds differ in the relevant kinds they comprise. I say "relevant" rather than "natural" for two reasons: first, "natural" is an inapt term to cover not only biological species but such artificial kinds as musical works, psychological experiments, and types of machinery; and second, "natural" suggests some absolute categorical or psychological priority, while the kinds in question are rather habitual or traditional or devised for a new purpose.

## (b) Weighting

While we may say that in the cases discussed some relevant kinds[14] of one world are missing from another, we might perhaps better say that the two worlds contain just the same classes sorted differently into relevant and irrelevant kinds.

---

[13] Discussion of what this means occupies many sections, from about Sec. 142 on, of Ludwig Wittgenstein's *Philosophical Investigations*, translated by G. E. M. Anscombe, (Blackwell, 1953). I am not suggesting that the answer I give here is Wittgenstein's.

[14] I speak freely of kinds here. Concerning ways of nominalizing such talk, see *SA*:II and *PP*:IV.

Some relevant kinds of the one world, rather than being absent from the other, are present as irrelevant kinds; some differences among worlds are not so much in entities comprised as in emphasis or accent, and these differences are no less consequential. Just as to stress all syllables is to stress none, so to take all classes as relevant kinds is to take none as such. In one world there may be many kinds serving different purposes; but conflicting purposes may make for irreconcilable accents and contrasting worlds, as may conflicting conceptions of what kinds serve a given purpose. Grue cannot be a relevant kind for induction in the same world as green, for that would preclude some of the decisions, right or wrong, that constitute inductive inference.

Some of the most striking contrasts of emphasis appear in the arts. Many of the differences among portrayals by Daumier, Ingres, Michelangelo, and Rouault are differences in aspects accentuated. What counts as emphasis, of course, is departure from the relative prominence accorded the several features in the current world of our everyday seeing. With changing interests and new insights, the visual weighting of features of bulk or line or stance or light alters, and yesterday's level world seems strangely perverted—yesterday's realistic calendar landscape becomes a repulsive caricature.

These differences in emphasis, too, amount to a difference in relevant kinds recognized. Several portrayals of the same subject may thus place it according to different categorial schemata. Like a green emerald and a grue one, even if the same emerald, a Piero della Francesca *Christ* and a Rembrandt one belong to worlds organized into different kinds.

Works of art, though, characteristically illustrate rather than name or describe relevant kinds. Even where the ranges of application—the things described or depicted—coincide, the features or kinds exemplified or expressed may be very different. A line drawing of softly draped cloth may exemplify rhythmic linear patterns; and a poem with no words for sadness and no mention of a sad person may in the quality of its language be sad and poignantly express sadness. The distinction between saying or representing on the one hand and showing or exemplifying on the other becomes even more evident in the case of abstract painting and music and dance that have no subject-matter but nevertheless manifest—exemplify or express—forms and feelings. Exemplification and expression, though running in the opposite direction from denotation—that is, from the symbol to a literal or metaphorical feature of it instead of to something the symbol applies to—are no less symbolic referential functions and instruments of worldmaking.[15]

Emphasis or weighting is not always binary as is a sorting into relevant and irrelevant kinds or into important and unimportant features. Ratings of relevance, importance, utility, value often yield hierarchies rather than dichotomies. Such weightings are also instances of a particular type of ordering.

## (c) Ordering

Worlds not differing in entities or emphasis may differ in ordering; for example, the worlds of different constructional systems differ in order of derivation. As nothing is at rest or is in motion apart from a frame of reference, so nothing is primitive or is derivationally prior to anything apart from a constructional system. However, derivation unlike motion is of little immediate practical interest; and thus in our everyday world, although we almost always adopt a frame of reference at least temporarily, we seldom adopt a derivational basis. Earlier I said that the difference between a world having points as pairs of lines and a world having lines as composed of points is that the

---

[15] On exemplification and expression as referential relations see *LA*, pp. 50–57, 87–95.

latter but not the former admits as entities nonlinear elements comprised within lines.  But alternatively we may say that these worlds differ in their derivational ordering of lines and points of the not-derivationally-ordered world of daily discourse.

Orderings of a different sort pervade perception and practical cognition.  The standard ordering of brightness in color follows the linear increase in physical intensity of light, but the standard ordering of hues curls the straight line of increasing wavelength into a circle.  Order includes periodicity as well as proximity; and the standard ordering of tones is by pitch and octave.  Orderings alter with circumstances and objectives.  Much as the nature of shapes changes under different geometries, so do perceived patterns change under different orderings; the patterns perceived under a twelve-tone scale are quite different from those perceived under the traditional eight-tone scale, and rhythms depend upon the marking off into measures.

Radical reordering of another sort occurs in constructing a static image from the input on scanning a picture, or in building a unified and comprehensive image of an object or a city from temporally and spatially and qualitatively heterogeneous observations and other items of information.[16]  Some very fast readers recreate normal word-ordering from a series of fixations that proceed down the left-hand page and then up the right-hand page of a book.[17]  And spatial order in a map or a score is translated into the temporal sequence of a trip or a performance.

All measurement, furthermore, is based upon order. Indeed, only through suitable arrangements and groupings can we han-

---

[16] See *The Image of the City* by Kevin Lynch (Cambridge, Technology Press, 1960).

[17] See E. Llewellyn Thomas, "Eye Movements in Speed Reading", in *Speed Reading: Practices and Procedures* (University of Delaware Press, 1962). pp. 104–114.

dle vast quantities of material perceptually or cognitively. Gombrich discusses the decimal periodization of historical time into decades, centuries, and millennia.[18] Daily time is marked off into twenty-four hours, and each of these into sixty minutes of sixty seconds each. Whatever else may be said of these modes of organization, they are not 'found in the world' but *built into a world*. Ordering, as well as composition and decomposition and weighting of wholes and kinds, participates in worldmaking.

## (d) Deletion and Supplementation

Also, the making of one world out of another usually involves some extensive weeding out and filling—actual excision of some old and supply of some new material. Our capacity for overlooking is virtually unlimited, and what we do take in usually consists of significant fragments and clues that need massive supplementation. Artists often make skillful use of this: a lithograph by Giacometti fully presents a walking man by sketches of nothing but the head, hands, and feet in just the right postures and positions against an expanse of blank paper; and a drawing by Katharine Sturgis conveys a hockey player in action by a single charged line.

That we find what we are prepared to find (what we look for or what forcefully affronts our expectations), and that we are likely to be blind to what neither helps nor hinders our pursuits, are commonplaces of everyday life and amply attested in the psychological laboratory.[19] In the painful experience of proofreading and the more pleasurable one of watching a skilled magician, we incurably miss something that is there and see something that is not there. Memory edits more ruthlessly; a

---

[18] In "Zeit, Zahl, und Zeichen", delivered at the Cassirer celebration in Hamburg, 1974.

[19] See "On Perceptual Readiness" (1957) in *BI*, pp. 7–42.

person with equal command of two languages may remember a learned list of items while forgetting in which language they were listed.[20]    And even within what we do perceive and remember, we dismiss as illusory or negligible what cannot be fitted into the architecture of the world we are building.

The scientist is no less drastic, rejecting or purifying most of the entities and events of the world of ordinary things while generating quantities of filling for curves suggested by sparse data, and erecting elaborate structures on the basis of meagre observations.    Thus does he strive to build a world conforming to his chosen concepts and obeying his universal laws.

Replacement of a so-called analog by a so-called digital system through the articulation of separate steps involves deletion; for example, to use a digital thermometer with readings in tenths of a degree is to recognize no temperature as lying between 90 and 90.1 degrees. Similar deletion occurs under standard musical notation, which recognizes no pitch between $c$ and $c\#$ and no duration between a sixty-fourth and a one hundred-and-twenty-eighth note. On the other hand, supplementation occurs when, say, an analog replaces a digital instrument for registering attendance, or reporting money raised, or when a violinist performs from a score.

Perhaps the most spectacular cases of supplementation, though, are found in the perception of motion.    Sometimes motion in the perceptual world results from intricate and abundant fleshing out of the physical stimuli.    Psychologists have long known of what is called the 'phi phemomenon': under carefully controlled conditions, if two spots of light are flashed a short distance apart and in quick succession, the viewer normally sees a spot of light moving continuously along a path from the first

---

[20] See Paul Kolers, "Bilinguals and Information Processing", *Scientific American* 218 (1968), 78–86.

position to the second. That is remarkable enough in itself since of course the direction of motion cannot have been determined prior to the second flash; but perception has even greater creative power. Paul Kolers has recently shown[21] that if the first stimulus spot is circular and the second square, the seen moving spot transforms smoothly from circle to square; and transformations between two-dimensional and three-dimensional shapes are often effected without trouble. Moreover, if a barrier of light is interposed between the two stimulus spots, the moving spot detours around the barrier. Just why these supplementations occur as they do is a fascinating subject for speculation (see further V below).

## (e) Deformation

Finally, some changes are reshapings or deformations that may according to point of view be considered either corrections or distortions. The physicist smooths out the simplest rough curve that fits all his data. Vision stretches a line ending with arrowheads pointing *in* while shrinking a physically equal line ending with arrowheads pointing *out*, and tends to expand the size of a smaller more valuable coin in relation to that of a larger less valuable one.[22] Caricaturists often go beyond overemphasis to actual distortion. Picasso starting from Velasquez's *Las Meninas*, and Brahms starting from a theme of Haydn's, work magical variations that amount to revelations.

These then are ways that worlds are made. I do not say *the* ways. My classification is not offered as comprehensive or clearcut or mandatory. Not only do the processes illustrated of-

---

[21] *Aspects of Motion Perception* (Pergamon Press, 1972), pp. 47ff.

[22] See "Value and Need as Organizing Factors in Perception" (1947), in *BI*, pp. 43–56.

ten occur in combination but the examples chosen sometimes fit equally well under more than one heading; for example, some changes may be considered alternatively as reweightings or reorderings or reshapings or as all of these, and some deletions are also matters of differences in composition. All I have tried to do is to suggest something of the variety of processes in constant use. While a tighter systematization could surely be developed, none can be ultimate; for as remarked earlier, there is no more a unique world of worlds than there is a unique world.

## 5. Trouble with Truth

With all this freedom to divide and combine, emphasize, order, delete, fill in and fill out, and even distort, what are the objectives and the constraints? What are the criteria for success in making a world?

Insofar as a version is verbal and consists of statements, truth may be relevant. But truth cannot be defined or tested by agreement with 'the world'; for not only do truths differ for different worlds but the nature of agreement between a version and a world apart from it is notoriously nebulous. Rather— speaking loosely and without trying to answer either Pilate's question or Tarski's—a version is taken to be true when it offends no unyielding beliefs and none of its own precepts. Among beliefs unyielding at a given time may be long-lived reflections of laws of logic, short-lived reflections of recent observations, and other convictions and prejudices ingrained with varying degrees of firmness. Among precepts, for example, may be choices among alternative frames of reference, weightings, and derivational bases. But the line between beliefs and precepts is neither sharp nor stable. Beliefs are framed in concepts informed by precepts; and if a Boyle ditches his data for a smooth curve just missing them all, we may say either that observational volume and pressure are different properties from theoretical volume and pressure or that the truths about volume and pressure differ in the two worlds of observation and theory. Even the staunchest belief may in time admit alternatives; "The earth is at rest" passed from dogma to dependence upon precept.

Truth, far from being a solemn and severe master, is a docile and obedient servant. The scientist who supposes that he is single-mindedly dedicated to the search for truth deceives himself. He is unconcerned with the trivial truths he could grind out endlessly; and he looks to the multifaceted and irregular results of observations for little more than suggestions of overall structures and significant generalizations. He seeks system, simplicity, scope; and when satisfied on these scores he tailors truth to fit (*PP*:VII, 6–8). He as much decrees as discovers the laws he sets forth, as much designs as discerns the patterns he delineates.

Truth, moreover, pertains solely to what is said, and literal truth solely to what is said literally. We have seen, though, that worlds are made not only by what is said literally but also by what is said metaphorically, and not only by what is said either literally or metaphorically but also by what is exemplified and expressed—by what is shown as well as by what is said. In a scientific treatise, literal truth counts most; but in a poem or novel, metaphorical or allegorical truth may matter more, for even a literally false statement may be metaphorically true (*LA*, pp. 51, 68–70) and may mark or make new associations and discriminations, change emphases, effect exclusions and additions. And statements whether literally or metaphorically true or false may show what they do not say, may work as trenchant literal or metaphorical examples of unmentioned features and feelings. In Vachel Lindsay's *The Congo*, for example, the pulsating pattern of drumbeats is insistently exhibited rather than described.

Finally, for nonverbal versions and even for verbal versions without statements, truth is irrelevant. We risk confusion when we speak of pictures or predicates as "true of" what they depict or apply to; they have no truth-value and may represent or denote some things and not others, while a statement does have truth-value and is true of everything if of anything.[23]  A nonrepresentational picture such as a Mondrian says nothing, denotes nothing, pictures nothing, and is neither true nor false, but shows much. Nevertheless, showing or exemplifying, like denoting, is a referential function; and much the same considerations count for pictures as for the concepts or predicates of a theory: their relevance and their revelations, their force and their fit—in sum their *rightness*. Rather than speak of pictures as true or false we might better speak of theories as right or wrong; for the truth of the laws of a theory is but one special feature and is often, as we have seen, overridden in importance by the cogency and compactness and comprehensiveness, the informativeness and organizing power of the whole system.

"The truth, the whole truth, and nothing but the truth" would thus be a perverse and paralyzing policy for any worldmaker. The whole truth would be too much; it is too vast, variable, and clogged with trivia. The truth alone would be too little, for some right versions are not true—being either false or neither true nor false—and even for true versions rightness may matter more.

---

[23] E.g., "$2+2=4$" is true of everything in that for every $x$, $x$ is such that $2+2=4$. A statement $S$ will normally not be *true about* $x$ unless $S$ is about $x$ in one of the senses of "about" defined in "About" (*PP*, pp. 246–272); but definition of "about" depends essentially on features of statements that have no reasonable analogues for pictures. See further: Joseph Ullian and Nelson Goodman, "Truth about Jones", *Journal of Philosophy*, Vol. 74 (1977), pp. 317–338; also VII:5 below.

## 6. Relative Reality

Shouldn't we now return to sanity from all this mad proliferation of worlds? Shouldn't we stop speaking of right versions as if each were, or had, its own world, and recognize all as versions of one and the same neutral and underlying world? The world thus regained, as remarked earlier, is a world without kinds or order or motion or rest or pattern—a world not worth fighting for or against.

We might, though, take the real world to be that of some one of the alternative right versions (or groups of them bound together by some principle of reducibility or translatability) and regard all others as versions of that same world differing from the standard version in accountable ways. The physicist takes his world as the real one, attributing the deletions, additions, irregularities, emphases of other versions to the imperfections of perception, to the urgencies of practice, or to poetic license. The phenomenalist regards the perceptual world as fundamental, and the excisions, abstractions, simplifications, and distortions of other versions as resulting from scientific or practical or artistic concerns. For the man-in-the-street, most versions from science, art, and perception depart in some ways from the familiar serviceable world he has jerry-built from fragments of scientific and artistic tradition and from his own struggle for survival. This world, indeed, is the one most often taken as real; for reality in a world, like realism in a picture, is largely a matter of habit.

Ironically, then, our passion for *one* world is satisfied, at different times and for different purposes, in *many* different ways. Not only motion, derivation, weighting, order, but even reality is relative. That right versions and actual worlds are many does not obliterate the distinction between right and wrong versions, does not recognize merely possible worlds answering to wrong versions, and does not imply that all right alternatives are equally good for every or indeed for any purpose. Not even a fly is likely to take one of its wing-tips as a fixed point; we do not welcome molecules or concreta as elements of our everyday world, or combine tomatoes and triangles and typewriters and tyrants and tornadoes into a single kind; the physicist will count none of these among his fundamental particles; the painter who sees the way the man-in-the-street does will have more popular than artistic success. And the same philosopher who here metaphilosophically contemplates a vast variety of worlds finds that only versions meeting the demands of a dogged and deflationary nominalism suit his purposes in constructing philosophical systems.

Moreover, while readiness to recognize alternative worlds may be liberating, and suggestive of new avenues of exploration, a willingness to welcome all worlds builds none. Mere acknowledgement of the many available frames of reference provides us with no map of the motions of heavenly bodies; acceptance of the eligibility of alternative bases produces no scientific theory or philosophical system; awareness of varied ways of seeing paints no pictures. A broad mind is no substitute for hard work.

## 7. Notes on Knowing

What I have been saying bears on the nature of knowledge. On these terms, knowing cannot be exclusively or even primarily a matter of determining what is true. Discovery often amounts, as when I place a piece in a jigsaw puzzle, not to arrival at a proposition for declaration or defense, but to finding a fit. Much of knowing aims at something other than true, or any, belief. An increase in acuity of insight or in range of comprehension, rather than a change in belief, occurs when we find in a pictured forest a face we already knew was there, or learn to distinguish stylistic differences among works already classified by artist or composer or writer, or study a picture or a concerto or a treatise until we see or hear or grasp features and structures we could not discern before. Such growth in knowledge is not by formation or fixation or belief [24] but by the advancement of understanding. [25]

Furthermore, if worlds are as much made as found, so also knowing is as much remaking as reporting. All the processes of worldmaking I have discussed enter into knowing. Perceiving motion, we have seen, often consists in producing it. Discovering laws involves drafting them. Recognizing patterns is very much a matter of inventing and imposing them. Comprehension and creation go on together.

I shall return in Chapters VI and VII to many of the questions surveyed here. Now I want to consider two much more specific topics: in Chapter II, a subtle categorization peculiarly significant for the arts; and in Chapter III, a sample tracing of a notion across versions in various systems and media.

---

[24] I allude here to Charles S. Peirce's paper, "The Fixation of Belief" (1877), in *Collected Papers of Charles Sanders Peirce*, Vol. 5 (Harvard University Press, 1934), pp. 223–247.

[25] On the nature and importance of understanding in the broader sense, see M. Polanyi, *Personal Knowledge* (University of Chicago Press, 1960).

# II

# The Status of Style

## 1. Exceptions Taken

Obviously, subject is what is said, style is how. A little less obviously, that formula is full of faults. Architecture and nonobjective painting and most of music have no subject. Their style cannot be a matter of how they say something, for they do not literally say anything; they do other things, they mean in other ways. Although most literary works say something, they usually do other things, too; and some of the ways they do some of these things are aspects of style. Moreover, the what of one sort of doing may be part of the how of another. Indeed, even where the only function in question is saying, we shall have to recognize that some notable features of style are features of the matter rather than the manner of the saying. In more ways than one, subject is involved in style. For this and other reasons, I cannot subscribe to the received opinion[1] that style depends upon an artist's conscious choice among alternatives. And I think we shall also have to recognize that not all differences in ways of writing or painting or composing or performing are differences in style.

---

[1] E.g., Stephen Ullmann, *Style in the French Novel* (Cambridge, 1957), p. 6, writes: "There can be no question of style unless the speaker or writer has the possibility of choosing between alternative forms of expression. Synonymy, in the widest sense of the term, lies at the root of the whole problem of style." This passage is quoted, with approval, by E. H. Gombrich in "Style", *International Encyclopedia of the Social Sciences*, Vol. 15, p. 353.

My quarrels, though, are not with the practice of critics and art historians but with their definitions and theories of style, so often at odds with that practice.[2]

## 2. Style and Subject

Plainly, when something is said, some aspects of the way it is said are matters of style. So far as the descriptive, narrative, or expository function of literature goes, variations in style are variations in how this function is performed by texts. Form varies while content remains constant—but there are difficulties with even this dictum. Graham Hough writes: "...the more we reflect on it, the more doubtful it becomes how far we can talk about different ways of saying; is not each different way of saying in fact the saying of a different thing?"[3] More recently, E. D. Hirsch, Jr., starting from the premiss that style and stylistics depend upon there being alternative ways of saying exactly the same thing, strives to defend and define synonymy.[4]

Synonymy is a suspect notion, and a study of my own suggests that no two terms have exactly the same meaning.[5] But distinctness of style from content requires not that exactly

---

[2] Useful suggestions concerning this chapter have been made by Howard Gardner, Vernon Howard, David Perkins, Sheldon Sacks, and Paolo Valesio.

[3] Graham Hough, in his admirable and useful *Style and Stylistics* (London, 1969), p. 4. I concur also with his skepticism about resurrecting the notion of synonymy through transformational linguistics.

[4] E. D. Hirsch, Jr., "Stylistics and Synonymity", *Critical Inquiry*, Vol. 1 (March 1975), pp. 559–579.

[5] Nelson Goodman, "On Likeness of Meaning," (1949) *PP*, pp. 231–238. This challenge to synonymy was by no means the first but (1) went further than earlier ones by showing that even under an analysis dependent solely on the extensions of terms, every two terms differ in meaning, and (2) suggested a criterion for comparative likeness of meaning, thus providing a basis for distinguishing style from content.

the same thing may be said in different ways but only that what is said may vary nonconcomitantly with ways of saying. Pretty clearly there are often very different ways of saying things that are very nearly the same. Conversely, and often more significantly, very different things may be said in much the same way—not, of course, by the same text but by texts that have in common certain characteristics that constitute a style. Many works on many matters may be in the same style; and much discussion of styles is carried on without regard to subject. Styles of saying—as of painting or composing or performing— may often be compared and contrasted irrespective of what the subjects are and even of whether there are any. Even without synonymy, style and subject do not become one.[6]

So far our results are negative and nearly nil. Not only is style not subject; but where there is no subject, style is not at all delimited by not being subject. Even this is a risky statement. For sometimes style *is* a matter of subject. I do not mean merely that subject may influence style but that some differences in style consist entirely of differences in what is said. Suppose one historian writes in terms of military conflicts, another in terms of social changes; or suppose one biographer stresses public careers, another personal lives. The differences between the two histories of a given period, or between the two biographies of a given person, here lie not in the character of the prose but in what is said. Nevertheless, these are differences in literary style no less pronounced than are differences in wording. I have purposely picked examples of descriptive or expository literature, but part of a poet's style as well may consist

---

[6] "Subject" is rather ambiguous as between topic and what is said about a topic; and some remarks below bear on the relationship between the two. But for purposes of the present chapter, differences among topic, subject, subject matter, content, what is said and what is named or described or depicted usually count for less than the shared differences from other features discussed below.

of what he says—of whether he focuses on the fragile and transcendent or the powerful and enduring, upon sensory qualities or abstract ideas, and so on.

The prospect of paradox looms here. If what is said is sometimes an aspect of style, and style is a way of saying what is said, a tactless logician might point to the unwelcome consequence that what is said is sometimes an aspect of a way of saying what is said—a formula with the ambivalent aroma of a self-contradictory truism.

The remedy looks at first sight even more weird. What is said, rather than being a way of saying what is said, may be a way of talking about something else; for example, writing about Renaissance battles and writing about Renaissance arts are not different ways of writing about the battles or about the arts but different ways of writing about the Renaissance. Saying different things may count as different ways of talking about something more comprehensive that embraces both. Thus without departing from the principle that style pertains to ways of saying we can, for example, recognize as aspects of style both writing about the battles rather than the arts and writing in Latinate rather than Anglo-Saxon prose.  But then we give up what seemed the very point of that principle: the contrast between ways of saying and what is said, between style and subject. If both packaging and contents are matters of style, what isn't?

Looking once more and harder, we may notice that differences in style dependent upon differences in subject do not arise from the mere fact that what is said is not the same. When the military-minded historian writes about two different periods, his style may remain the same even though what he says is very different—at least as different as what he and the arts-minded historian write about a given period. To say that style is a matter of subject is thus vague and misleading. Rather, only *some* features of what is said count as aspects of style; only certain characteristic differences in what is said constitute differences in style.

Likewise, of course, only certain features of the wording, and not others, constitute features of style. That two texts consist of very different words does not make them different in style. What counts as features of style here are such characteristics as the predominance of certain kinds of words, the sentence structure, and the use of alliteration and rhyme.

Thus we need not have worried about the difficulty of distinguishing form from content;[7] for that distinction, insofar as it is clear at all, does not coincide with but cuts across the distinction between what is style and what is not. Style comprises certain characteristic features both of what is said and of how it is said, both of subject and of wording, both of content and of form. The distinction between stylistic and nonstylistic features has to be drawn on other grounds.

## 3. Style and Sentiment

Have we by any chance in our struggle so far, left out the very essence of style? Some say that style enters where fact stops and feeling starts; that style is a matter of the 'affective and expressive'[8] as against the logical, intellectual, cognitive aspects of art; that neither what is said nor what says it have anything to do with style except as they participate in expressing emotion. Two reports of a walk in the rain that use different words and describe different incidents may be in the same style, but they are in different styles if one is glum and the other gleeful. Style in general on this view consists of such, and much more subtle,

---

[7] And in view of VII:2 below, that is just as well.

[8] E.g., C. Bally; see the account of his view in Hough, especially p. 23.

qualities of feeling expressed.

As a criterion for distinguishing stylistic from nonstylistic features, this proposal has obvious limitations. Under any plausible sorting of properties into emotive and cognitive, some stylistic properties are emotive and some are not. Tight or loose construction, brevity or verbosity, plain or ornate vocabulary may arouse but hardly express admiration or antipathy and are surely not themselves emotional properties. Accordingly, "emotion" in this context comes to be replaced by the vaguer term "feeling"; and each plainly nonemotive stylistic property is held to have its peculiar feel. Periodic sentences feel different from loose sentences; we can feel the difference between a Latinate and an Anglo-Saxon vocabulary. Moreover, we are often aware of these qualities of feeling before we discern the underlying factual properties, as we often feel a pain before perceiving the wound. And it is just these feelings rather than their vehicles that count as aspects of style. Such is the claim.

In this version, the thesis is attenuated to the point of evaporation. In any sense that the cited features of a text have their peculiar feeling qualities, so it seems does every other—indeed every word and sequence of words. That we can feel such properties seems to mean little more than that we can perceive them without analysis into component traits, just as we recognize a face; but this surely is true of most properties, and useless for distinguishing style. Making the theory broad enough is making it too broad to work.

Furthermore, definition of style in terms of feelings expressed goes wrong in overlooking not only structural features that are neither feelings nor expressed but also features that though not feelings *are* expressed. Although the Sturgis drawing and the Pollaiuolo engraving illustrated below (pp. 30 and 31) both represent men in physical conflict, the Sturgis expresses flashing action while the Pollaiuolo expresses poised power.[9] A Daumier lithograph may express weight, a passage from Vivaldi express visual or kinaesthetic patterns of skaters, and Joyce's *Ulysses* express an infinite cycling of time.

Thus style is confined neither to what is expressed nor to feelings. Nevertheless, expressing is at least as important a function of many works as is saying; and what a work expresses is often a major ingredient of its style. The differences between sardonic, sentimental, savage, and sensual writing are stylistic. Emotions, feelings, and other properties expressed in the saying are part of the way of saying; what is expressed is an aspect of how what is said is said, and as in music and abstract painting may be an aspect of style even when nothing is said.

All this is plain enough, and yet plainly not enough. For since expression is a function of works of art, *ways* of expressing as well as ways of saying must be taken into account. And as differences in what is expressed may count as differences in style of saying, so differences in what is said may count as differences in style of expressing. Gloominess may be typical of a writer's way of describing outdoor activities; emphasis on rainy weather may be typical of his way of expressing gloom. What is said, how it is said, what is expressed, and how it is expressed are all intimately interrelated and involved in style.

## 4. Style and Structure

That features of what is said and of what is expressed must be taken into account does not at all diminish the central importance of sentence structure, rhythmic pattern, use of iteration and antithesis, and so on. Nor, as illustrated by certain characteristics of vocabulary (Latinate or Anglo-Saxon, collegiate or

---

[9] Both works, of course, express much else.

Katharine Sturgis. Drawing from a hockey series. Ink. Courtesy of the artist.

colloquial) in prose and of color in painting, are all features of
style that are not properties of what is said or expressed 'formal'
or 'structural' in any but an overstretched sense.

We are tempted to classify all such properties as intrinsic or internal on the ground that unlike properties of something—
subject or feeling—that a text or picture refers to by way of
denotation (description, representation, etc.) or expression,
these belong to, are possessed by, are inherent in, the text or
picture itself. But philosophers have had trouble trying to draw
any clear line between internal and external properties. After
all, what a text says or expresses is a property of the text, not of
something else; and on the other hand, properties possessed by
the text are different from and are not enclosed within it, but
relate it to other texts sharing these properties.

Antonio Pollaiuolo, *Battle of Naked Men*. Engraving. Courtesy of the Cleveland Museum of Art. Purchase, J. H. Wade Fund.

Can this class of not exclusively formal and not clearly intrinsic features be better defined in terms of the difference between what a work *does* and what it *is?* Saying the earth is round or expressing gloom is doing so; being tautly written or freely painted is just being so. I am afraid this does not quite work either. In the first place, the gloom expressed by a poem or picture is in my view possessed by it, albeit metaphorically rather than literally; that is, the poem or picture expressing gloom *is* (metaphorically) gloomy.[10] In the second place, I think the so-called in-

---

[10] Even though a metaphorical statement may be literally false, metaphorical truth differs from metaphorical falsity much as literal truth differs from literal falsity. This and other matters—pertaining to metaphor, to denotation and exemplification and expression, and to symbolization or reference in general—that are essential to but can only be briefly summarized in the present chapter are more fully explained in *LA*:II.

trinsic stylistic features of a work are never merely possessed but are among those possessed properties that are manifested, shown forth, *exemplified*—just as color and texture and weave, but not shape or size, are exemplified by the tailor's swatch he uses as a sample. Thus, expressing and exemplifying alike are matters of being and doing, of possessing properties *and* referring to them. This, indeed, provides a clue to the distinction we have been trying to make: the features here in question, whether structural or nonstructural, are all properties literally exemplified by a work.

Exemplification, though one of the most frequent and important functions of works of art, is the least noticed and understood. Not only some troubles about style but many futile debates over the symbolic character of art can be blamed on ignoring the lessons, readily learned from everyday cases of the relation of being-a-sample-of, that mere possession of a property does not amount to exemplification, that exemplification involves reference by what possesses to the property possessed, and thus that exemplification though obviously different from denotation (or description or representation) is no less a species of reference.

In summary so far, a feature of style may be a feature of what is said, of what is exemplified, or of what is expressed. Goya and El Greco characteristically differ in all three ways: in subject matter, drawing, and feeling. Features of any of these kinds may also be ways of performing one or more of the three functions. For example, shapes exemplified in a painting of drapery may at once constitute a way of representing costume and a way of expressing bulk or agitation or dignity; the drapery "can curl, it can swirl, it can billow, it can melt; or it can resist the eye with a structure of humps and hollows as durable as a rock modelled by the waves," can become "an instrument of harmonious certainty."[11] In other cases, differences in what is expressed—say in

---

[11] Quotations are from Kenneth Clark, *Piero della Francesca*, 2d ed. (London, 1969), p. 14.

the character of the risen Christ in Mantegna's engraving and Piero della Francesca's painting—may be different ways of depicting the same subject. Again, features of what is said may be ways of saying or expressing; Whitman's choice of detail is both an aspect of his way of describing human beings and his way of celebrating vitality, and the different subjects chosen by Vermeer and de Heem and van der Heyden and van Everdingen are at once different ways of depicting life in seventeenth-century Holland and different ways of expressing its domestic quality. Sometimes, features of what is exemplified, such as color organizations, are ways of exemplifying other features, such as a spatial pattern; witness the differently colored impressions from a single silk-screen design by Albers, and more recently by Patrick Heron. And a given structure, such as the sonnet form, may of course be exemplified in poems having quite different subjects, so that features of a subject matter count as ways of exemplifying a form.

But we need not ring all the changes here or argue over particular examples. My purpose has not been to impose an elaborate and rigid system of classification upon features of style, but rather to free the theory of style from the warping constraints of prevalent dogma—from the misleading opposition of style and subject, of form and content, of what and how, of intrinsic and extrinsic. Far from claiming that the tripartite taxonomy outlined is mandatory or the best possible or even altogether adequate, I am urging explicit recognition of aspects of style that, while often considered by critics, are shortchanged by traditional theory. This does not answer but only underlines the question what in general distinguishes stylistic features from others? Identifying the properties of a literary—or pictorial or musical—style matters more than further classifying them into ways of saying, exemplifying, and expressing.

## 5. Style and Signature

Yet while style embraces features of the several sorts described, such features are not always stylistic. If a work is in a given style, only certain among all the aspects of the subject, form, and feeling of the work are elements of that style.

In the first place, a property—whether of statement made, structure displayed, or feeling conveyed—counts as stylistic only when it associates a work with one rather than another artist, period, region, school, etc. A style is a complex characteristic that serves somewhat as an individual or group signature—that bespeaks Resnais or Whistler or Borodin, that distinguishes early from late Corot, Baroque from Rococo, Baoulé from Pahouin. By extension, we may speak of a work by one author as being in the style of another, or of a passage being or not being in the style of other passages in the same or another work; but in general stylistic properties help answer the questions: who? when? where? A feature that is nonindicative by itself may combine with others to place a work; a property common to many works may be an element of style for some but stylistically irrelevant for others; some properties may be only usual rather than constant features of a given style; and some may be stylistically significant not through appearing always or even often in works of a given author or period but through appearing never or almost never in other works. No fixed catalogue of the elementary properties of style can be compiled; and we normally come to grasp a style without being able to analyze it into component features. The test of our grasp lies in the sureness and sensitivity of our sorting of works.

In the second place, not even every property that helps determine the maker or period or provenance of a work is stylistic. The label on a picture, a listing in a catalogue raisonné, a letter from the composer, a report of excavation may help place a work; but being so labelled or documented or excavated is not a matter of style. Nor are the chemical properties of pigments that help identify a painting. Even being signed by Thomas Eakins or Benjamin Franklin is an identifying property that is not stylistic. Although a style is metaphorically a signature, a literal signature is no feature of style.

Why do such properties, even though plainly who-when-where relevant, fail to qualify as stylistic? Briefly, because they are not properties of the functioning of the work as a symbol. In contrast, such typical stylistic qualities as a concentration upon setting, a peculiar elaboration of curved forms, a subtle quality of bittersweet feeling, are aspects of what the poem or picture or piano sonata says or exemplifies or expresses. Style has to do exclusively with the symbolic functioning of a work as such.[12] Earlier we saw that any, and now we see that only, aspects of such symbolic functioning may enter into a style.

The lineaments of a definition of style are thus before us. Basically, the style consists of those features of the symbolic functioning of a work that are characteristic of author, period, place, or school. If this definition does not seem notably novel, still its divergence from some prevalent views must not be overlooked. According to this definition, style is not exclusively a matter of how as contrasted with what, does not depend either upon synonymous alternatives or upon conscious choice among alternatives, and comprises only but not all aspects of how and what a work symbolizes.

Throughout, I have been speaking of style of works of art. But need style, as conceived here, be confined to works, or might the term "work" in our definition be as well replaced by "object" or by "anything"? Unlike some other definitions, ours

---

[12] And only as such; not, for example, with the symbolic functioning of a poem as a message in some military code.

does not rest upon an artist's intentions. What counts are properties symbolized, whether or not the artist chose or is even aware of them; and many things other than works of art symbolize. Insofar as the properties in question are characteristic of an author or maker, style indeed pertains only to artefacts, unless "maker" covers also the person who presents an *objet trouvé* as art. But natural objects and events may function otherwise as symbols, and properties of what they symbolize may be characteristic of time or place of origin or occurrence. A Mandalay sunrise may be not merely a sunrise in Mandalay but a sunrise expressing the suddenness of thunder—a sunrise in Mandalay style. Nevertheless, in the present context we may do well to restrict "style" to works and performances and objects of art.[13]

Some stylistic features are more prominent and more telling than others; but the line between trivial stylistic features and features like those cited earlier that are not stylistic at all has seldom been clearly drawn. Consider some fussy statistical characteristic of the novels of a given author, such as that more than the usual proportion of second words of his sentences begin with consonants. Is the difference between this and an important genuine feature of style categorical or comparative? This property is statistical, but so are many plainly stylistic properties such as the frequency of rhyme or alliteration. This property is determinable only by long labor; but some of the most significant properties of style are so subtle as to be discovered only at great pains. Finally, that this property is too *ad hoc* to be interesting is a matter of degree; just as

---

[13] Although my examples in the present paper are works, what I say of styles applies equally to performances. The much-abused question "What is art?"—that is how, or better when, anything qualifies as a work of art, good or bad—and related questions concerning the *objet trouvé* and conceptual art are explored once more in IV below.

generalizations in science are the more *ad hoc* the fewer and weaker their connections with the theoretical background, so stylistic properties are the more *ad hoc* the fewer and weaker their connections with the network of other stylistic concepts.

So far, then, nothing distinguishes our preposterous property from unmistakably stylistic properties. Nevertheless, our definition of style discloses a categorical difference here. Though our property indeed belongs to the novels in question and even identifies them as by the given author, it is hardly exemplified or symbolized in any way by them as works. In this it is like the size and shape of a tailor's swatch that serves as a sample not of these properties but of color and texture. Since our property is not symbolized by the novels, it does not satisfy our definition of style. In contrast with even the strangest or most negligible stylistic properties, this is not a stylistic property at all.

Now admittedly, while what is or is not exemplified by a tailor's swatch is evident enough, just which properties are exemplified by a work of art or a performance is often difficult to determine. The distinction drawn in the definition may sometimes be hard to apply. But likewise, we often find it hard to tell just what a work says or expresses. That we have trouble making a determination implies that there is something to be determined: that the work in fact does or in fact does not say so-and-so, does or does not exemplify (or express) a given property. Whether a property is stylistic depends no more than what a work says either upon the difficulty of determining or upon the importance of what is exemplified or said.

### 6. The Significance of Style

Stylistics, plainly, is a narrow part of criticism. Criticism may incorporate discussion not only of historical, biographical, psychological, and sociological factors, but of any properties whatever of the works studied. Stylistics, in contrast, is confined to features of what and how the works symbolize, and still further to such of these features as are characteristic of a given author, period, region, school, etc.

Does this mean that concepts of style are mere instruments for the literary or art historian, curatorial devices for sorting works according to origin? Are styles, like catalogue listings and excavation reports, simply aids in filing or have they aesthetic significance? Is stylistics merely part of the mechanics of scholarship or does it concern works as art?

The question as framed is misleading. It assumes that attribution is alien to aesthetics, that the 'mere' identification of artist, period, place, or school is aesthetically irrelevant, that history and criticism are entirely independent pursuits. This is a mistake. As I have argued elsewhere (*LA*:III, 1 and 2), knowledge of the origin of a work, even if obtained by chemical analysis or other purely scientific means, informs the way the work is to be looked at or listened to or read, providing a basis for the discovery of nonobvious ways the work differs from and resembles other works. Indeed the perceptual discovery of a style must usually start from prior identification of works representing an artist or school. Thus attributions however effected contribute to the understanding of works as art.

The question really at issue here is different: whether stylistic properties have any more direct aesthetic significance than do nonstylistic properties that aid attribution. The answer is implicit in what has already been said. Placing a work is itself aesthetically significant insofar as it makes for discovery of such qualities as those of style. That style is by definition characteristic of an author or period or region or school does not reduce it to a device for attribution; rather, so far as aesthetics is concerned, attribution is a preliminary or auxiliary to or a byproduct of the perception of style. History and criticism differ not in having separate subject matters or unrelated tasks but in exchanging ends for means. Where the historian uses his grasp of style to identify a picture as by Rembrandt or a poem as by Hopkins, the critic uses the identification of authorship as a step toward discerning the Rembrandt properties or the Hopkins properties of the work.

Why, though, should style matter more than some quality that might be discerned, with enough study, as characteristic of works in a random selection? Partly for the same reason that *ad hoc* stylistic properties count for little: lack of interesting interrelationships with the ever developing fabric of other features involved in organizing our aesthetic experience; and partly because, in the absence of any claimed correlation with such projectible factors as authorship or school, our tentative perception cannot be reinforced, refined, or extended by testing against further cases.[14] Nothing here is incompatible with the familiar fact that interesting qualities are sometimes revealed through the juxtaposition of works in a mixed anthology, exhibition, collection, or concert, or even a storeroom jumble.

The style of Haydn or Hardy or Holbein does not proclaim itself to the casual listener or reader or museum goer, and is seldom to be recognized by following explicit instructions. Styles are normally accessible only to the knowing eye or ear, the tuned sensibility, the informed and inquisitive mind. This is not surprising, or even peculiar to styles. No feature of anything is so central or so potentially prominent as not to be overlooked even under close and repeated scrutiny. What we find, or succeed in making, is heavily dependent on how and what we seek. As noted earlier, we may fail to see the face in a picture puzzle. We may miss form and feeling as we focus upon what is

---

[14] See further below, VII: 6 and 7.

said, or miss what is said as we listen to rhyme and rhythm. If we are equally at home in two languages, we may hardly notice and quickly forget which words we hear or read are in which language. Overall design may be ignored for or distract attention from fine detail. The perception of any pattern not fitting the structure of the search often takes great trouble.

Yet the more complicated and elusive the style, the more does it stimulate exploration and reward success with illumination. An obvious style, easily identified by some superficial quirk, is properly decried as a mere mannerism. A complex and subtle style, like a trenchant metaphor, resists reduction to a literal formula. We usually perceive the style or the sadness of a picture or a poem without being able to analyze either property into elements or specify necessary and sufficient conditions for it. Just for this reason, the perception when achieved increases the dimensions of our comprehension of the work. The less accessible a style is to our approach and the more adjustment we are forced to make, the more insight we gain and the more our powers of discovery are developed. The discernment of style is an integral aspect of the understanding of works of art and the worlds they present.

# III

# Some Questions
# Concerning Quotation

### 1. Verbal Quotation

Philosophers of language have paid some attention in recent years to the nature of direct quotation, especially in discussions warning against confusion between use and mention, and perhaps even more attention to the proper interpretation of indirect quotation. Virtually all this work has been confined exclusively to linguistic or verbal quotation. What about quotation of other sorts? If a string of words can quote another string of words, can a picture quote a picture, or a symphony quote another symphony? And if I can quote your words can I also quote, or only imitate or describe, your gestures?

Before we examine such questions about nonverbal quotation, we might do well to review what we know about verbal quotation, starting with the following sentence:

*A1.* triangles have three sides.

The truth of this doesn't matter; but I have purposely chosen a tenseless statement—a statement such that all its replicas have the same truth-value—so that we need not distinguish among the different replicas.

By putting quotation marks around *A1*, we make a name for it that also *directly quotes* it:

*A2.* "triangles have three sides".

Note that *A2*, unlike *A1*, is not a sentence, but a name. Of course, we might name or describe *A1* without quoting it, e.g. by

*A3.* item *A1*.

Or we might, by prefixing *A1* with a "that", indirectly quote it:

*A4.* that triangles have three sides.

Now *A2* both names and contains *A1*; *A3* names but does not contain *A1*. What about *A4*? It happens to contain *A1*; but *A1* can also be indirectly quoted by an expression that does not contain it, e.g.:

*A5.* that three-angled polygons have three straight boundaries; or
*A5'.* que les triangles ont trois bords.

But does *A4* or *A5* name *A1*? Not at all; *A4* and *A5* are rather *predicates* applying to *A1* and to all paraphrases[1] of it. *A4*, for example, is elliptical for "expression to the effect that triangles have three sides".

In summary:

*A2* both names and contains *A1*
*A3* names but does not contain *A1*
*A4* contains but does not name *A1*
*A5* neither contains nor names *A1*.

That is, a direct quotation of a sentence both names and contains it; an indirect quotation does not name and need not contain it. For symmetry, we may also note that of course an ex-

---

[1]In dealing with indirect quotation, I adopt Israel Scheffler's treatment and terminology. See his "An Inscriptional Approach to Indirect Quotation", *Analysis*, Vol. 14 (1954), pp. 83–90, and "Inscriptionalism and Indirect Quotation", *Analysis*, Vol. 19 (1958), pp. 12–18.

pression may contain *A1* without quoting it either directly or indirectly; e.g.:

*A6.* No triangles have three sides such that any two are parallel.

Looking over this summary, we may wonder a little why both *A2* and *A5* are considered to be quotations of some sort, while *A3* and *A6* are not. For direct quotation, both naming and containment are necessary.[2] At least one of these requirements is met by *A3* and *A6*, but neither is met by *A5*. Yet we associate *A5* with *A2* by calling both quotations. Is there any good reason for this?

Perhaps the explanation is that both *A2* and *A5* refer to—more particularly, denote—*A1*, and that both contain some paraphrase of *A1*, since every expression is of course a paraphrase of itself. Apparently two necessary conditions for quotation, direct or indirect, are *(a) containment* of some paraphrase of what is quoted, and *(b) reference* to what is quoted, by either naming or predication. On this account, rather than indirect quotation getting its name by widening the application of "quotation" beyond direct or proper quotation, direct quotation becomes a special case of indirect quotation. But this unifying formula must not be allowed to hide an important difference. The relation required in direct quotation between what is quoted and what is contained is syntactic identity or, if we take what is quoted as an utterance or inscription rather than as a universal type, is syntactic replication—sameness of spelling.[3] On the other hand, the relation required in indirect quotation is semantic paraphrasis—some sort of equivalence of reference or of meaning.

---

[2] I do not say these are *sufficient* conditions; indeed, we shall see later that as they stand they are not.

[3] Concerning utterances, inscriptions, and replicas see *SA*:XI, 1 and 2. Concerning the general notion of sameness of spelling see *LA*: IV, 2.

Incidentally, while a name (for example, "Pegasus") may be fictive, naming nothing, and a predicate may be empty, applying to nothing, the names and predicates that are quotations cannot be fictive or empty. A name that is a direct quotation cannot be fictive, for it contains what it names; and a predicate that is an indirect quotation cannot be empty, for it contains one of the paraphrases it applies to.

What is quoted need not, of course, be a sentence. A word, a syllable, a letter, even a punctuation mark, can be quoted. Parallels of *A1–A3*, for instance, are:

*B1.* tree
*B2.* "tree"
*B3.* item *B1.*

But what is the parallel of *A4*? Since *A4* is a predicate applying to all paraphrases of *A1*, what we want here is a predicate applying to all paraphrases of "(is a) tree". Parallels of *A4–A6* are:

*B4.* tree term
*B5.* term for large woody plants
*B5'.* mot pour les arbres
*B6.* a tree is not a poem.

If what is quoted is a letter or a nonsense syllable rather than a word, parallels of *A1–A3* are again obvious:

*C1.* t
*C2.* "t"
*C3.* item *C1*;

but we are at a loss to find a parallel of *A4*. Sometimes suggested are predicates such as "(is a) tee" or "20th letter of the alphabet" that apply to all instances of the letter "t". But instances or replicas of a letter are not paraphrases of it; for the relation of paraphrase, as we have seen, is a semantic one, depending upon reference or meaning. A paraphrase of a term applies to what the term applies to; a paraphrase of a sentence restates what the sentence says. But a letter that is not a word or a sentence is without reference or meaning, and has no paraphrases. Thus there are *no* parallels here of *A4–A5'*. As a parallel of *A6* any word containing the letter will do, e.g.

*C6*.  at.

The situation differs in an interesting way for "Pegasus" even though this word, like the letter "t", does not denote anything. Parallel to *A1–A3* are:

*D1*.  Pegasus
*D2*.  "Pegasus"
*D3*.  item D1;

but is there a parallel for *A4* as there is for "tree", or none as for "t"? If "tree-term" means merely "expression having the same extension as 'tree' ", then the notion of a paraphrase for "Pegasus" is as gratuitous as the notion of a paraphrase for "t". But "Pegasus" unlike "t" is a word belonging to the category of names, and the results of compounding it with such other words as "picture" or "description" are terms that have non-null extensions. The extensions of such compound terms are secondary extensions[4] of "Pegasus".

Now we have a parallel of *A4* and *B4* in

*D4*.  Pegasus-term,

applying to all paraphrases of "Pegasus", where a paraphrase of

---

[4]Concerning the notion of secondary extensions see my papers "On Likeness of Meaning" (1949) and "On Some Differences about Meaning" (1953), *PP*: V, 2 and 3.

a term preserves not only the primary but also the requisite[5] secondary extensions of that term. In short, "Pegasus" can be paraphrased because though devoid of primary it is not devoid of secondary extensions—because, in popular parlance, it is not meaningless. Similarly, parallels of *A5–A6* are:

*D5*. Bellerophon's-winged-horse term
*D5'*. mot pour le cheval ailé de Bellerophon
*D6*. wing of Pegasus.

So far, we have been discussing verbal or linguistic quotation exclusively; and we have found that two necessary conditions for such quotation, direct or indirect, are:

(*a*) containment of what is quoted or of some other replica or paraphrase of it, and

(*b*) reference to—by naming or predication of—what is quoted.

These conditions are not, we must note, sufficient. The term

*E*. the twentieth letter of the alphabet

both denotes and contains but surely does not quote the letter described. We thus need to add some such requirement for direct quotation as this:

(*c*) replacement of the denoted and contained expression by any other of the language results in an expression that denotes the replacing expression.

Obviously, replacing what is within quotation marks will satisfy this requirement, but putting in some other letter (or word, etc.) for the described letter in the above description will not; the usual result will be nonsense, such as

*F*. fhe fwenfief leffer of fhe alphabef.

---

[5]Preservation of *all* secondary extensions would be too strong a demand; see the papers cited in note 4 above.

## 2. Pictorial Quotation

When do we have quotation in nonverbal systems? Let us start with picturing and with direct quotation. When does a picture directly quote another?

Clearly, mere containment of one picture in another no more constitutes quotation than does containment of one expression in another as in *A6*, *B6*, etc. A double portrait does not quote the contained portraits; a seascape does not quote the picture of a ship in it.

Nor, again, does reference to a picture by another constitute quotation. Suppose that in a painting of a museum gallery only the edge of Rembrandt's *Night Watch* is shown, or the *Night Watch* is shown with heads of viewers blocking out parts of it. This painting is a picture of, refers to, the *Night Watch* but does not quote—because it does not contain—it. A picture directly quotes another only if it both refers to and contains it. But what are the means by which a picture refers to another that it contains? In other words, what is the pictorial analogue of quotation marks?

Fairly obviously, as quotation marks are put around an expression to quote it directly, a picture of a frame may be put around a picture to quote it directly; and there are other devices, such as painting it as on an easel, or as hanging on a wall, that work in the same way. But now we face a peculiar difficulty. If I want to paint a picture directly quoting the *Night Watch*, I can hardly put the *Night Watch* itself into my canvas and paint a frame around it. Does the containment requirement imply that a picture can quote only what is actually within it? That would surely be too severe a demand.

Look back again at *A1* and *A2*. We noticed that *A2* contains *A1* if we take them as universals or types, but that if we take them as particular inscriptions we should rather say that *A2* (or that every replica of it) contains some replica of *A1*. The *inscription A2* above does not contain the *inscription A1*, but rather a replica of that inscription.

The trouble in the case of paintings, though, is that (unlike expressions) they belong to what I call a *singular* symbol system.[6] Each painting is unique; in the technical sense of *replica*, there are no replicas of pictures as there are replicas of words. We must remember that being a replica and being a copy are quite different matters; replicas may differ drastically so long as they are spelled the same way. Since picturing has no alphabet and no notational criterion for sameness of spelling, direct verbal quotation has no strict analogue in painting.

A photograph, on the other hand, is not unique. Photographic picturing is a multiple symbol system. The relation among the several prints from a negative is to some extent comparable to the relation among the several replicas of a word; but the two relations are not the same. In the first case we have an autographic and in the second an allographic symbol system; that is, the relation among the prints consists in their having been produced from the same negative while the relation among the inscriptions consists in their being spelled the same way. Still, since both systems are multiple, with their symbols having plural instances, 'duplication' among the prints might be accepted as a tolerable even though admittedly inexact analogue of replication among the inscriptions. Then a photograph may actually contain a duplicate of a second photograph; and the first, if it also refers to the second through showing it as in a frame, etc., might then be said to quote it directly.

---

[6]Concerning *singular*, *multiple*, *autographic*, and *allographic* symbol systems, see *LA*: III, 3 and 4.

Returning to paintings and drawings, can we justify stretching the analogy still further by using some notion of "copy" in place of "duplicate" or "replica"? That would stretch the analogy very thin indeed since, as we have seen, copying as a relation in an autographic singular symbol system differs drastically from replication as a relation in an allographic multiple one. Once we start stretching an analogy, though, where we stop is rather arbitrary. All I am inclined to say here is that what we consider to be direct pictorial quotation will depend upon what we are willing to take as an adequate analogue of replication in direct verbal quotation.

What about indirect pictorial quotation? Can we find a pictorial analogue of a predicate applying to all paraphrases of a picture? The generality called for here gives no trouble. A picture may refer not to a particular picture but to many pictures, may be a picture not of the *Night Watch* but of group pictures in general or of Rembrandt pictures in general,[7] and so on. Also, perhaps we could somehow so construe *pictorial copy* as to make it analogous enough to *paraphrase*. But then we face the troublesome question: if a painted frame is a pictorial analogue of quotation marks, what is a pictorial analogue for the "that" (or for the "-term") of indirect quotation? The answer, I suspect, may be that the distinction between direct and indirect quotation is not so sharp in picturing as in language, and that a painted frame may function as an analogue either of quotation marks or of "that", with only the context, if anything, determining which. English might easily have included some likewise ambiguous device, say

---

[7]On general representations, see *LA*: I, 5, and my reply to Monroe Beardsley in *Erkenntnis*, Vol. 12 (1978), pp. 169–173.

$$\{ \qquad \}$$

such that

John said { triangles have three sides }

would be noncommittal as to whether John uttered the particular words in question or only uttered some paraphrase of them. Unless the context resolves the ambiguity in favor of the direct-quotation interpretation, the effect is that of indirect quotation. To some extent, indeed, the "that" of English is likewise capable of being so affected by context as to have the force of quotation marks; e.g., in

John said in just these words that triangles have three sides.

## 3. Musical Quotation[8]

The problems concerning musical quotation are quite different. Let us confine ourselves here to music that, whether traditional or not, is scored in traditional notation. The notation defines replica-hood: two performances of the same score, however else they may differ, count as replicas of each other. Thus there is no difficulty about one musical event containing a replica of another.

The problem here is rather with reference. No more than in language does mere containment constitute quotation; but what in music makes the difference between merely containing a replica of a passage and referring to that passage? In other words, what in music is the analogue of quotation marks? The answer, as matters stand, seems to be "nothing". Curiously, of the two requirements for quotation, the containment condition gives

---

[8]I have profited from several discussions with Vernon Howard on this topic.

trouble for pictures while the reference condition gives trouble for music.

That music has no analogue for quotation marks seems, though, rather an accident. Nothing stands in the way of introducing into musical notation characters, even ordinary quotation marks themselves, to function as quotation marks.[9] If these marks are not played—i.e., if they have no sound-compliants—the analogy with language is very close; for quotation marks in language are unpronounced; they occur in writing but not in speaking. In spoken English, we do not distinguish between these two:

(a) John said triangles have three sides
(b) John said "triangles have three sides".

What we say or hear may be an utterance of either (a), which is elliptical for

(c) John said that triangles have three sides,

or of (b). While we can resolve the doubt in one way by putting in a "that"—which, unlike quotation marks, is pronounced—we cannot in English as it stands resolve the doubt in the other way. Of course, some clues by way of context, emphasis, and pause may help; for example, if in the above case "said" is stressed and followed by a noticeable pause, direct quotation is clearly indicated. And such clues, sufficiently standardized, might constitute an auditory device for direct quotation in language or in music.

Perhaps the reason we do not in fact, though we easily might, have unsounded quotation marks in musical notation is that in music the sound is the end product. In English, on the contrary,

---

[9]I am told that some composers have used quotation marks in just this way but I cannot cite examples.

what is written is no mere means to what is said but is of at least equal importance in its own right; the fact that some things written are unspoken does not make them superfluous.

As for indirect quotation in music, what could be the analogue of paraphrase? *Paraphrase of*, as noted, is a semantic relation; and music most often has no denotation. A term is paraphrased by another having the same primary extension and (depending upon the discourse) certain of the same secondary extensions. But music that has no extension can no more be paraphrased than can a letter or nonsense syllable. The inevitable suggestion that *transposition* or *variation* is a musical analogue of paraphrase is obviously wrong; for musical transposition and variation are syntactic rather than semantic relations, resting upon relationships of notes and patterns themselves rather than upon anything they denote.[10]

Where music is descriptive, does denote, paraphrase takes on meaning. But for indirect quotation, which requires an analogue of a predicate applying to all paraphrases of a given passage, we further need a musical analogue of the "that" or the "-term" in English. Since the latter, unlike quotation marks, *are* sounded, the mere addition to musical notation of some unsounded sign would not quite do here. Indirect quotation in music can be effected if at all by means of sound cues, just as in spoken English when the "that" is suppressed.

## 4. Cross-System Quotation

That what is quoted and what quotes sometimes belong to different systems has already been illustrated. The predicates of

---

[10]Vernon Howard has made the interesting suggestion that if we take paraphrase as a matter of preserving reference in general, exemplificational as well as denotational, a musical *variation* might perhaps be construed as paraphrase in the sense of preserving exemplificational reference. See his "On Musical Quotation" in *The Monist*, Vol. 58 (1974), pp. 307-318.

indirect quotation quite obviously cover paraphrases not only in English but in other languages as well. Only so could such a statement as

Jean said that triangles have three sides

be true if Jean spoke in French.

Furthermore, an expression of any language may be directly quoted in English by enclosure within quotation marks. A foreign expression combines with the surrounding quotation marks to give a term *in English*—an English name of the quoted expression. As Alonzo Church has insisted,[11] such a sentence as

Jean a dit "Les triangles ont trois bords"

is properly translated into English by

John said "Les triangles ont trois bords"

and *not* by

Jean said "Triangles have three sides",

which incorrectly reports Jean as having uttered a sentence of English.

Of course, when a French novel is translated into English, the dialogue as well as the rest of the text is put into English. This literary rather than literal use of quotation marks results in something between direct and indirect quotation. Here, in contrast with literal direct quotation, what quotes does not contain what is quoted; but in contrast with indirect quotation, what is contained must be not merely a paraphrase but a translation of what is quoted—and translation is a narrower relation than paraphrasis.

---

[11]See his paper "On Carnap's Analysis of Statements of Assertion and Belief" *Analysis*, Vol. 10 (1950), pp. 97–99.

Consider the pictorial analogue of this looser 'literary' sort of quotation. Suppose a picture, done according to standard Western conventions of perspective, shows a Japanese print hanging on the wall. The contained print, as required for quotation in the stricter sense, is drawn according to Oriental conventions. The analogue of translating into English what is within quotation marks in a French novel would here consist in translating the Japanese print into Western perspective! The analogy for music is obvious.

If words from any other language can be quoted in English, can symbols from nonlinguistic systems likewise be quoted in English? Subject to the reservations above discussed concerning even pictorial quotation of pictures, a picture (like a foreign word) combines with surrounding quotation marks in an English text to make an English term. In contrast, if pictures (or foreign words) occur without quotation marks, the text is no longer in English but in a mixture of systems.

Furthermore, since paraphrases may be in any language, little stands in the way of admitting nonlinguistic paraphrases as well. If we suppose (*contra* VII,5 below) that pictures make statements, then in

John affirmed that the clouds are full of angels,

the predicate beginning with "that" may be construed as applying to pictorial as well as to verbal paraphrases of

the clouds are full of angels.

John may have uttered words in English or in Turkish or have painted a picture. Often, of course, the context restricts the application of the predicate, for example, to linguistic paraphrases if "affirmed" is replaced by "said", or to pictorial paraphrases if "affirmed" is replaced by "proclaimed in paint".

As pictures may be thus quoted directly or indirectly in

language, so may linguistic expressions be quoted by pictures. A familiar instance is a motto shown in a picture of a Victorian room. The painted frame combines with the contained words, say

Home, Sweet Home

to make a pictorial, not a verbal, symbol. One might, alternating between pictorial and verbal systems, then quote in English the pictorial quotation of the English motto, then quote in a picture the resulting verbal quotation, and so on.

In sum, a visual system that has means for quoting its own symbols normally has means for quoting other visual symbols.

## 5. Cross-Modal Quotation

While an English text that quotes a picture or foreign words remains English, and a picture that quotes words remains a picture, how could a picture quote sound, or sound quote a picture? Plainly, sound can be contained in a picture, or a picture contained in sound, only if the notion of containment is stretched beyond any pertinent limit.

Yet we are brought up short by the recognition that spoken English is readily quoted in writing, and written English in speech. The gap between sight and sound, though seemingly too great to be bridged by quotation (which involves containment) is bridged casually in everyday discourse.

The explanation lies in the close correspondence between inscriptions and utterances of the same expression. Indeed, utterances and inscriptions of an expression have equal status as instances of it; they may be considered replicas of each other. Replicas, so long as the spelling is the same, may differ in appearance or sound or even in medium (*LA*:IV, 7). Just for this reason, I can quote in writing what John said, or quote in speech what he wrote. But auditory and pictorial symbols in general stand in no such determinate relation to one another.

The nearest analogy to language in this respect can be found in music. The relationship between a score and its performance, although a semantic relationship between symbol and compliant rather than a syntactic relationship between replicas in different media, is as determinate as that between a written and a spoken word. Thus, much as we may quote speech in writing by enclosing the written correlate in quotation marks, so may we quote musical sound on paper by putting the score in quotation marks. And a picture showing a sheet of score is to this extent quoting also the sounded music. Again, if John says "It went like this" and then hums the opening of Beethoven's Fifth, he might be regarded as in effect quoting the score as well as the sound.

## 6. Reflection

The question concerning the quotation of gestures, raised at the end of my opening paragraph, I leave to the reader's reflection.

My goal in this chapter has not been to find in or force upon nonlinguistic systems strict analogies with quotation in languages. There was no hope or need for such strict analogies. Rather, I have undertaken a comparative study of quotation and its nearest analogues. As ways of combining and constructing symbols, these are among the instruments for world-making.

# IV

# When Is Art?

## 1. The Pure in Art

If attempts to answer the question "What is art?" characteristically end in frustration and confusion, perhaps—as so often in philosophy—the question is the wrong one. A reconception of the problem, together with application of some results of
a study of the theory of symbols, may help to clarify such moot
matters as the role of symbolism in art and the status as art of
the 'found object' and so-called 'conceptual art'.

One remarkable view of the relation of symbols to works of
art is illustrated in an incident bitingly reported by Mary Mc-
Carthy:[1]

Seven years ago, when I taught in a progressive college, I had a pretty
girl student in one of my classes who wanted to be a short-story writer.
She was not studying with me, but she knew that I sometimes wrote
short stories, and one day, breathless and glowing, she came up to me in
the hall, to tell me that she had just written a story that her writing
teacher, a Mr. Converse, was terribly excited about. "He thinks it's won-
derful" she said, "and he's going to help me fix it up for publication."
I asked what the story was about; the girl was a rather simple being
who loved clothes and dates. Her answer had a deprecating tone. It was
about a girl (herself) and some sailors she had met on the train. But then
her face, which had looked perturbed for a moment, gladdened.

---

[1] "Settling the Colonel's Hash", *Harper's Magazine*, 1954; reprinted in *On
the Contrary* (Farrar, Straus and Cudahy, 1961), p. 225.

"Mr. Converse is going over it with me and we're going to put in the symbols."

Today the bright-eyed art student will more likely be told, with equal subtlety, to keep out the symbols; but the underlying assumption is the same: that symbols, whether enhancements or distractions, are extrinsic to the work itself. A kindred notion seems to be reflected in what we take to be symbolic art. We think first of such works as Bosch's *Garden of Delight* or Goya's *Caprichos* or the Unicorn tapestries or Dali's drooping watches, and then perhaps of religious paintings, the more mystical the better. What is remarkable here is less the association of the symbolic with the esoteric or unearthly than the classification of works as symbolic upon the basis of their having symbols as their subject matter—that is, upon the basis of their depicting rather than of being symbols. This leaves as nonsymbolic art not only works that depict nothing but also portraits, still-lifes, and landscapes where the subjects are rendered in a straightforward way without arcane allusions and do not themselves stand as symbols.

On the other hand, when we choose works for classification as nonsymbolic, as art without symbols, we confine ourselves to works without subjects; for example, to purely abstract or decorative or formal paintings or buildings or musical compositions. Works that represent anything, no matter what and no matter how prosaically, are excluded; for to represent is surely to refer, to stand for, to symbolize. Every representational work is a symbol; and art without symbols is restricted to art without subject.

That representational works are symbolic according to one usage and nonsymbolic according to another matters little so long as we do not confuse the two usages. What matters very much, though, according to many contemporary artists and critics, is to isolate the work of art as such from whatever it symbolizes or refers to in any way. Let me set forth in quotation marks, since I am offering it for consideration without now expressing any opinion of it, a composite statement of a currently much advocated program or policy or point of view:

"What a picture symbolizes is external to it, and extraneous to the picture as a work of art. Its subject if it has one, its references—subtle or obvious—by means of symbols from some more or less well-recognized vocabulary, have nothing to do with its aesthetic or artistic significance or character. Whatever a picture refers to or stands for in any way, overt or occult, lies outside it. What really counts is not any such relationship to something else, not what the picture symbolizes, but what it is in itself—what its own intrinsic qualities are. Moreover, the more a picture focuses attention on what it symbolizes, the more we are distracted from its own properties. Accordingly, any symbolization by a picture is not only irrelevant but disturbing. Really pure art shuns all symbolization, refers to nothing, and is to be taken for just what it is, for its inherent character, not for anything it is associated with by some such remote relation as symbolization."

Such a manifesto packs punch. The counsel to concentrate on the intrinsic rather than the extrinsic, the insistence that a work of art is what it is rather than what it symbolizes, and the conclusion that pure art dispenses with external reference of all kinds have the solid sound of straight thinking, and promise to extricate art from smothering thickets of interpretation and commentary.

## 2. A Dilemma

But a dilemma confronts us here. If we accept this doctrine of the formalist or purist, we seem to be saying that the content of such works as the *Garden of Delight* and the *Caprichos* doesn't really matter and might better be left out. If we reject the doctrine, we seem to be holding that what counts is not just what a work is but lots of things it isn't. In the one case we seem to be advocating lobotomy on many great works; in the other we seem to be condoning impurity in art, emphasizing the extraneous.

The best course, I think, is to recognize the purist position as all right and all wrong. But how can that be? Let's begin by agreeing that what is extraneous is extraneous. But is what a symbol symbolizes always external to it? Certainly not for symbols of all kinds. Consider the symbols:

(a) "this string of words", which stands for itself;
(b) "word", which applies to itself among other words;
(c) "short", which applies to itself and some other words and many other things; and
(d) "having seven syllables", which has seven syllables.

Obviously what some symbols symbolize does not lie entirely outside the symbols. The cases cited are, of course, quite special ones, and the analogues among pictures—that is, pictures that are pictures of themselves or include themselves in what they depict can perhaps be set aside as too rare and idiosyncratic to carry any weight. Let's agree for the present that what a work represents, except in a few cases like these, is external to it and extraneous.

Does this mean that any work that represents nothing meets the purist's demands? Not at all. In the first place, some surely symbolic works such as Bosch's paintings of weird monsters, or the tapestry of a unicorn, represent nothing; for there are no such monsters or demons or unicorns anywhere but in such pictures or in verbal descriptions. To say that the tapestry 'represents a unicorn' amounts only to saying that it is a unicorn-picture, not that there is any animal, or anything at all that it portrays.[2] These works, even though there is nothing they represent, hardly satisfy the purist. Perhaps, though, this is just another philosopher's quibble; and I won't press the point. Let's agree that such pictures, though they represent nothing, are representational in character, hence symbolic and so not 'pure'. All the same, we must note in passing that their being representational involves no representation of anything outside them, so that the purist's objection to them cannot be on that ground. His case will have to be modified in one way or another, with some sacrifice of simplicity and force.

In the second place, not only representational works are symbolic. An abstract painting that represents nothing and is not representational at all may express, and so symbolize, a feeling or other quality, or an emotion or idea.[3] Just because expression is a way of symbolizing something outside the painting—which does not itself sense, feel or think—the purist rejects abstract expressionist as well as representational works.

For a work to be an instance of 'pure' art, of art without symbols, it must on this view neither represent nor express nor even be representational or expressive. But is that enough? Granted, such a work does not stand for anything outside it; all it has are its own properties. But of course if we put it that way, all the properties any picture or anything else has—even such a property as that of representing a given person—are properties of the picture, not properties outside it.

---

[2] See further "On Likeness of Meaning" (1949) and "On Some Differences about Meaning" (1953), *PP*, pp. 221–238; also *LA*, pp. 21–26.

[3] Motion, for instance, as well as emotion may be expressed in a black and white picture; for example, see the pictures in II:4 above. Also see the discussion of expression in *LA*, pp. 85–95.

The predictable response is that the important distinction among the several properties a work may have lies between its internal or intrinsic and its external or extrinsic properties; that while all are indeed its own properties, some of them obviously relate the picture to other things; and that a nonrepresentational, nonexpressive work has only internal properties.

This plainly doesn't work; for under any even faintly plausible classification of properties into internal and external, any picture or anything else has properties of both kinds. That a picture is in the Metropolitan Museum, that it was painted in Duluth, that it is younger than Methuselah, would hardly be called internal properties. Getting rid of representation and expression does not give us something free of such external or extraneous properties.

Furthermore, the very distinction between internal and external properties is a notoriously muddled one. Presumably the colors and shapes in a picture must be considered internal; but if an external property is one that relates the picture or object to something else, then colors and shapes obviously must be counted as external; for the color or shape of an object not only may be shared by other objects but also relates the object to others having the same or different colors or shapes.

Sometimes, the terms "internal" and "intrinsic" are dropped in favor of "formal". But the formal in this context cannot be a matter of shape alone. It must include color, and if color, what else? Texture? Size? Material? Of course, we may at will enumerate properties that are to be called formal; but the 'at will' gives the case away. The rationale, the justification, evaporates. The properties left out as nonformal can no longer be characterized as all and only those that relate the picture to something outside it. So we are still faced with the question what if any *principle* is involved—the question how the properties that matter in a nonrepresentational, nonexpressive painting are distinguished from the rest.

I think there is an answer to the question; but to approach it, we'll have to drop all this high-sounding talk of art and philosophy, and come down to earth with a thud.

## 3. Samples

Consider again an ordinary swatch of textile in a tailor's or upholsterer's sample book. It is unlikely to be a work of art or to picture or express anything. It's simply a sample—a simple sample. But what is it a sample of? Texture, color, weave, thickness, fiber content....; the whole point of this sample, we are tempted to say, is that it was cut from a bolt and has all the same properties as the rest of the material. But that would be too hasty.

Let me tell you two stories—or one story with two parts. Mrs. Mary Tricias studied such a sample book, made her selection, and ordered from her favorite textile shop enough material for her overstuffed chair and sofa—insisting that it be exactly like the sample. When the bundle came she opened it eagerly and was dismayed when several hundred 2" x 3" pieces with zigzag edges exactly like the sample fluttered to the floor. When she called the shop, protesting loudly, the proprietor replied, injured and weary, "But Mrs. Tricias, you said the material must be exactly like the sample. When it arrived from the factory yesterday, I kept my assistants here half the night cutting it up to match the sample."

This incident was nearly forgotten some months later, when Mrs. Tricias, having sewed the pieces together and covered her furniture, decided to have a party. She went to the local bakery, selected a chocolate cupcake from those on display and ordered enough for fifty guests, to be delivered two weeks later. Just as the guests were beginning to arrive, a truck drove up with a single huge cake. The lady running the bake-shop was utterly discouraged by the complaint. "But Mrs. Tricias, you have no idea how much trouble we went to. My husband runs the textile shop and he warned me that your order would have to be in one piece."

The moral of this story is not simply that you can't win, but that a sample is a sample of some of its properties but not others. The swatch is a sample of texture, color, etc. but not of size or shape. The cupcake is a sample of color, texture, size, and shape, but still not of all its properties. Mrs. Tricias would have complained even more loudly if what was delivered to her was like the sample in having been baked on that same day two weeks earlier.

Now in general which of its properties is a sample a sample of? Not all its properties; for then the sample would be a sample of nothing but itself. And not its 'formal' or 'internal' or, indeed, any one specifiable set of properties. The kind of property sampled differs from case to case: the cupcake but not the swatch is a sample of size and shape; a specimen of ore may be a sample of what was mined at a given time and place. Moreover, the sampled properties vary widely with context and circumstance. Although the swatch is normally a sample of its texture, etc. but not of its shape or size, if I show it to you in answer to the question "What is an upholsterer's sample?" it then functions not as a sample of the material but as a sample of an upholsterer's sample, so that its size and shape are now among the properties it is a sample of.

In sum, the point is that a sample is a sample of—or *exemplifies* —only some of its properties, and that the properties to which it bears this relationship of exemplification[4] vary with circum-

---

[4] For further discussion of exemplification, see *LA*, pp. 52–67.

stances and can only be distinguished as those properties that it serves, under the given circumstances, as a sample of. Being a sample of or exemplifying is a relationship something like that of being a friend; my friends are not distinguished by any single identifiable property or cluster of properties, but only by standing, for a period of time, in the relationship of friendship with me.

The implications for our problem concerning works of art may now be apparent. The properties that count in a purist painting are those that the picture makes manifest, selects, focuses upon, exhibits, heightens in our consciousness—those that it shows forth—in short, those properties that it does not merely possess but *exemplifies*, stands as a sample of.

If I am right about this, then even the purist's purest painting symbolizes. It exemplifies certain of its properties. But to exemplify is surely to symbolize—exemplification no less than representation or expression is a form of reference. A work of art, however free of representation and expression, is still a symbol even though what it symbolizes be not things or people or feelings but certain patterns of shape, color, texture that it shows forth.

What, then, of the purist's initial pronouncement that I said facetiously is all right and all wrong? It is all right in saying that what is extraneous is extraneous, in pointing out that what a picture represents often matters very little, in arguing that neither representation nor expression is required of a work, and in stressing the importance of so-called intrinsic or internal or 'formal' properties. But the statement is all wrong in assuming that representation and expression are the only symbolic functions that paintings may perform, in supposing that what a symbol symbolizes is always outside it, and in insisting that what counts in a painting is the mere possession rather than the exemplification of certain properties.

Whoever looks for art without symbols, then, will find none—if all the ways that works symbolize are taken into account. Art without representation or expression or exemplification—yes; art without all three—*no*.

To point out that purist art consists simply in the avoidance of certain kinds of symbolization is not to condemn it but only to uncover the fallacy in the usual manifestos advocating purist art to the exclusion of all other kinds. I am not debating the relative virtues of different schools or types or ways of painting. What seems to me more important is that recognition of the symbolic function of even purist painting gives us a clue to the perennial problem of when we do and when we don't have a work of art.

The literature of aesthetics is littered with desperate attempts to answer the question "What is art?" This question, often hopelessly confused with the question "What is good art?", is acute in the case of found art—the stone picked out of the driveway and exhibited in a museum—and is further aggravated by the promotion of so-called environmental and conceptual art. Is a smashed automobile fender in an art gallery a work of art? What of something that is not even an object, and not exhibited in any gallery or museum—for example, the digging and filling-in of a hole in Central Park as prescribed by Oldenburg? If these are works of art, then are all stones in the driveway and all objects and occurrences works of art? If not, what distinguishes what is from what is not a work of art? That an artist calls it a work of art? That it is exhibited in a museum or gallery? No such answer carries any conviction.

As I remarked at the outset, part of the trouble lies in asking the wrong question—in failing to recognize that a thing may function as a work of art at some times and not at others. In crucial cases, the real question is not "What objects are (permanently) works of art?" but "When is an object a work of art?"—or more briefly, as in my title, "When is art?"

My answer is that just as an object may be a symbol—for instance, a sample—at certain times and under certain circumstances and not at others, so an object may be a work of art at some times and not at others. Indeed, just by virtue of functioning as a symbol in a certain way does an object become, while so functioning, a work of art. The stone is normally no work of art while in the driveway, but may be so when on display in an art museum. In the driveway, it usually performs no symbolic function. In the art museum, it exemplifies certain of its properties—e.g., properties of shape, color, texture. The hole-digging and filling functions as a work insofar as our attention is directed to it as an exemplifying symbol. On the other hand, a Rembrandt painting may cease to function as a work of art when used to replace a broken window or as a blanket.

Now, of course, to function as a symbol in some way or other is not in itself to function as a work of art. Our swatch, when serving as a sample, does not then and thereby become a work of art. Things function as works of art only when their symbolic functioning has certain characteristics. Our stone in a museum of geology takes on symbolic functions as a sample of the stones of a given period, origin, or composition, but it is not then functioning as a work of art.

The question just what characteristics distinguish or are indicative of the symbolizing that constitutes functioning as a work of art calls for careful study in the light of a general theory of symbols. That is more than I can undertake here, but I venture the tentative thought that there are five symptoms of the aesthetic:[5] (1) syntactic density, where the finest differences in certain respects constitute a difference between

---

[5] See *LA*, pp. 252–255 and the earlier passages there alluded to. The fifth symptom has been added above as the result of conversations with Professors Paul Hernadi and Alan Nagel of the University of Iowa.

symbols—for example, an ungraduated mercury thermometer as contrasted with an electronic digital-read-out instrument; (2) semantic density, where symbols are provided for things distinguished by the finest differences in certain respects—for example, not only the ungraduated thermometer again but also ordinary English, though it is not syntactically dense; (3) relative repleteness, where comparatively many aspects of a symbol are significant—for example, a single-line drawing of a mountain by Hokusai where every feature of shape, line, thickness, etc. counts, in contrast with perhaps the same line as a chart of daily stockmarket averages, where all that counts is the height of the line above the base; (4) exemplification, where a symbol, whether or not it denotes, symbolizes by serving as a sample of properties it literally or metaphorically possesses; and finally (5) multiple and complex reference, where a symbol performs several integrated and interacting referential functions,[6] some direct and some mediated through other symbols.

These symptoms provide no definition, much less a full-blooded description or a celebration. Presence or absence of one or more of them does not qualify or disqualify anything as aesthetic; nor does the extent to which these features are present measure the extent to which an object or experience is aesthetic.[7] Symptoms, after all, are but clues; the patient may have the symptoms without the disease, or the disease without the symptoms. And even for these five symptoms to come somewhere near being disjunctively necessary and conjunctively (as a syndrome) sufficient might well call for some redrawing of the

---

[6] This excludes ordinary ambiguity, where a term has two or more quite independent denotations at quite different times and in quite different contexts.

[7] That poetry, for example, which is not syntactically dense, is less art or less likely to be art than painting that exhibits all four symptoms thus does not at all follow. Some aesthetic symbols may have fewer of the symptoms than some nonaesthetic symbols. This is sometimes misunderstood.

vague and vagrant borderlines of the aesthetic. Still, notice that these properties tend to focus attention on the symbol rather than, or at least along with, what it refers to. Where we can never determine precisely just which symbol of a system we have or whether we have the same one on a second occasion, where the referent is so elusive that properly fitting a symbol to it requires endless care, where more rather than fewer features of the symbol count, where the symbol is an instance of properties it symbolizes and may perform many interrelated simple and complex referential functions, we cannot merely look through the symbol to what it refers to as we do in obeying traffic lights or reading scientific texts, but must attend constantly to the symbol itself as in seeing paintings or reading poetry. This emphasis upon the nontransparency of a work of art, upon the primacy of the work over what it refers to, far from involving denial or disregard of symbolic functions, derives from certain characteristics of a work as a symbol.[8]

Quite apart from specifying the particular characteristics differentiating aesthetic from other symbolization, the answer to the question "When is art?" thus seems to me clearly to be in terms of symbolic function. Perhaps to say that an object is art when and only when it so functions is to overstate the case or to speak elliptically. The Rembrandt painting remains a work of art, as it remains a painting, while functioning only as a blanket; and the stone from the driveway may not strictly become art by functioning as art.[9] Similarly, a chair remains a chair even if never sat on, and a packing case remains a packing case even if

---

[8] This is another version of the dictum that the purist is all right and all wrong.

[9] Just as what is not red may look or be said to be red *at certain times*, so what is not art may function as or be said to be art at certain times. That an object functions as art at a given time, that it has the status of art at that time, and that it is art at that time may all be taken as saying the same thing—so long as we take none of these as ascribing to the object any stable status.

never used except for sitting on. To say what art does is not to say what art is; but I submit that the former is the matter of primary and peculiar concern. The further question of defining stable property in terms of ephemeral function—the what in terms of the when—is not confined to the arts but is quite general, and is the same for defining chairs as for defining objects of art. The parade of instant and inadequate answers is also much the same: that whether an object is art—or a chair—depends upon intent or upon whether it sometimes or usually or always or exclusively functions as such. Because all this tends to obscure more special and significant questions concerning art, I have turned my attention from what art is to what art does.

A salient feature of symbolization, I have urged, is that it may come and go. An object may symbolize different things at different times, and nothing at other times. An inert or purely utilitarian object may come to function as art, and a work of art may come to function as an inert or purely utilitarian object. Perhaps, rather than art being long and life short, both are transient.

The bearing that this inquiry into the nature of works of art has upon the overall undertaking of this book should by now have become quite clear. How an object or event functions as a work explains how, through certain modes of reference, what so functions may contribute to a vision of—and to the making of—a world.

# V

# A Puzzle about Perception

## 1. Seeing beyond Being

Once in awhile, someone asks me rather petulantly "Can't you see what's before you?" Well, yes and no. I see people, chairs, papers, and books that are before me, and also colors, shapes, and patterns that are before me. But do I see the molecules, electrons, and infrared light that are also before me? And do I see this state, or the United States, or the universe? I see only parts of the latter comprehensive entities, indeed, but then I also see only parts of the people, chairs, etc. And if I see a book, and it is a mess of molecules, then do I not see a mess of molecules? But, on the other hand, can I see a mess of molecules without seeing any of them? If I cannot be said to see a mess of molecules because "mess of molecules" is a sophisticated way of describing what I see, not arrived at by any simple look, then how could I be said to see a magnet or a poisonous mushroom? Suppose someone asks whether I saw the football coach at my lecture, and I say "No". But he was there in the audience and I surely saw everyone in the audience. Although I saw him, I say I didn't, because I didn't know that the man at the right end of the eighth row center was the football coach.

Already we are in danger of losing ourselves in an all-too-familiar tangle of not-too-clear questions. You will be glad to hear, and I am even gladder to say, that I shall not be dealing with such questions about seeing or not seeing what is before us but rather with some cases of seeing what is not before us.

## 2. Motion Made

That we often—and with considerable regularity and predictability—see what is not there should be evident enough from the optical illusions illustrated in psychological literature, from watching magicians, and from reading proof. What I want to discuss now, because it raises some intriguing theoretical problems, is the seeing of *motion* or *change* that is not there. My primary source is Paul A. Kolers, *Aspects of Motion Perception*.[1]

The simplest and best-known phenomenon of apparent motion occurs when a spot against a contrasting background is exposed very briefly, followed after an interval of from 10 to 45 milliseconds by exposure of a like spot a short distance away.[2] With a shorter time-interval at the same distance, we see two spots as flashed simultaneously; with a longer interval, we see the two spots flashed successively; but within the specified time-interval, we see one spot moving from the first position to the second. According to Kolers, this phenomenon was "a well-known laboratory curiosity" when Sigmund Exner first subjected it to formal experiment in 1875, but until the work of Max Wertheimer in 1910, it awaited more systematic study (*AMP*, 1–2). Kolers speculates that the delay

---

[1] Pergamon Press, Oxford, 1972. This book, hereafter referred to as *AMP*, is an outstanding document in experimental and theoretical psychology. My account of it here is fragmentary, but owes much to many discussions with Paul Kolers.

[2] Say 1.4°. For limits and variations in intervals and distances, as well as details of apparatus and procedure, see *AMP*, Chap. 3.

was due in part to a lack of suitable apparatus, but even more
to the resistance of "a mechanistic philosophy that argued
for a one-to-one correspondence between physical stimulation
and psychological experience. The phenomenon of apparent
motion is a dramatic violation of that assumed equivalence"
(*AMP*, 3). Unfortunately, dramatic violations often fail to
disturb dogma.

Nowadays this simplest and most commonplace case of
apparent motion raises no eyebrows. We casually attribute
it to some expected sort of neural arc-jumping, of retinal
or cortical short-circuiting. Actually, it poses some hard and
significant questions. In the first place, how much like the
perception of apparent motion is the perception of real motion,
where the spot actually moves from one place to the other?
In the latter case do we simply, rather than tracking the spot
all along the path, pick it up at a few places and fill in the
rest much as when no spot traverses the path? Are the 'motion-
detectors'[3] involved in apparent-motion perception as well as
in real-motion perception? If so are they detectors, rather, of
quick succession? If not, then visual motion does not always
depend on them. In the second place, how are we able in
the case of apparent motion to fill in the spot at the intervening
place-times along a path running from the first to the second
flash *before that second flash occurs?* How do we know
which way to go? One intriguing hypothesis, advanced by
van der Waals and Roelofs (*AMP*, 44), is that the intervening
motion is produced retrospectively, built only after the second

---

[3] See "What the Frog's Eye Tells the Brain", by J. Y. Lettvin, H. K. Maturana,
W. S. McCulloch, and W. H. Pitts, *Proceedings of the Institute of Radio Engineers*, Vol. 47, (New York, 1959), pp. 1940–1951. See further Sec. 4 and note 7
below.

flash occurs and projected backwards in time.[4]

Kolers in his book rejects both the analogy with real-motion perception and also the hypothesis of retrospective construction; but neither idea is so implausible or unappealing as to be given up easily, and we shall want to examine the arguments and the evidence later.

## 3. Shape and Size

Kolers began his experimental investigation by asking what happens when figures rather than dots or spots are successively flashed. Since a figure in some sense consists of many dots, we might well predict that when the same figure is flashed both times, it will be seen to move just as a dot does. But what if different figures are flashed, say a square first and then a triangle or a circle? Or suppose the two figures are the same in shape but different in size. Small differences of any sort we might expect to be bridged smoothly; but how great a difference is required to disrupt smooth transition and yield events apparently as well as physically separate? For example, is the difference between a small circle and a large cube enough, or is it more than enough?

When we put the question this way we are assuming that we already have the relevant measure of similarity to be used in determining the limits of dissimilarity for smooth apparent change. But while we do have an obvious measure for similarity of size where shape is constant, we do not have any such measure for similarity among different shapes. Is a circle more like a thin ellipse or a regular hexagon or a sphere? Is a cube more like a square or a tetrahedron? Is a long rectangle with a

---

[4] For further discussion of this matter, see Sec. 4 below.

tiny corner clipped off more like the unclipped rectangle or a regular pentagon? Any number of equally reasonable principles give different similarity-orderings of shapes.

Why not, then, reverse our stance and take two figures as the more similar according as they more readily and smoothly transform into one another? We glimpse here the pleasing prospect, which I discussed with Kolers early in his experimental study, of finding an empirically grounded measure, or at least gross comparative test, for psychological similarity of one important kind. Let me anticipate any more detailed report on the experiments by confessing that they dashed that happy hope when they showed that almost any difference between two figures is smoothly resolved. Apparent change is no responsive instrument for measuring similarity (*AMP*, 46 *ff*).

Obviously, the term "apparent *motion*" is far too narrow for the scope of the Kolers study, which examines apparent change of many kinds: change in position, in shape, in size, or in any two or all three of these. In some experiments, the successive flashes are superimposed on one another so that the apparent change involves growth or diminution or deformation or some combination of these without motion of the whole. While change in shape may often be said to involve motion of parts, this need not be true for growth or diminution. Furthermore, even "change" is too narrow to cover cases where flashes of the same figure are exactly superimposed; here the filling-in of the interval to give a single constant figure produces stability rather than change. The underlying general phenomenon operating in all these cases is the perceptual bridging or supplementation that builds a unified whole, fixed or moving, stable or changing.

As I have already intimated, the experiments show that within the time and distance limits specified, supplementation normally occurs between successive flashes joining them into one enduring and perhaps moving, growing, shrinking, or otherwise changing phenomenal whole whether the two stimulus figures are the same or differ drastically. This works so widely for plane and solid figures, physical objects, letters and other symbols, paired so heterogeneously, that such transformability yields no serviceable similarity classes of shapes. Kolers writes: "If all two-dimensional [and three dimensional][5] shapes are members of the same class, as they seem almost to be shown to be in the present results, . . . then the idea of establishing classes of shapes according to the visual operations performed upon them is hopeless" (*AMP*, 190). If these results pile up so unanimously as to begin to lose their novelty, we must still not overlook the ingenuity shown in improvising routes of resolution in some cases. I say "improvising" because the routes taken between the same two figures may vary considerably with circumstances, subjects, and occasions. For example, transition from a cube to a square may sometimes be accomplished by extraction and sometimes by compression; and transition from a trapezoid to its reversal, sometimes by planar transformation and sometimes by rotation in depth (*AMP*, 88–91).[6] Incidentally, some of us might look upon such improvisation as more characteristically 'human' than are innately implanted ideas. I have even wondered, quite irresponsibly, whether certain types of routing might correlate with certain aptitudes or other psychological characteristics well enough to provide a basis for some sort of diagnostic test.

---

[5] In view of the Kolers results, confinement to two-dimensional shapes here is gratuitous.

[6] And a single general description may allow for wide variation in route. For example, when Kolers here speaks of the trapezoids' "rotation on their horizontal axes through the third dimension" without further specification, the rotation may presumably occur in different directions on different occasions.

What happens, though, if a fixed barrier is interposed between the locations of the two flashes? Let us say that on a white field with a black line down the middle, a black circle is flashed first to the left of the line and then (within the temporal and spatial limits stipulated) to the right of it? Is apparent motion then entirely prevented or only interrupted? Neither, Kolers reports. The circle moves right, comes forward around the barrier, and continues to the second position (*AMP*, 79–80).

In all cases so far considered, each exposure is of a single figure or object. Kolers goes on to much more complex, sometimes startling, and often theoretically crucial cases. For example, in one experiment (*AMP*, 82) the successive exposures were of the two four-figure groups in Figure 1.

**Figure 1**

With the first group flashed at the left followed by the second group to the right of it, what route of transition is ordinarily followed? Since, when single figures are used, squares and circles easily transform into one another, won't each circle here become a square and each square a circle as the group moves right? Not at all. Instead, the right three figures of the first group, without changing shape, move as a unit to become the left three figures of the second, while the leftmost circle of the first group moves around to become the rightmost figure of the second! In a second experiment with the rightmost figure of the second group displayed replaced by a square, the leftmost circle of the first group changes to a square as it moves around to the right end.

Plainly the visual system is persistent, inventive, and sometimes rather perverse in building a world according to its own lights; the supplementation is deft, flexible, and often elaborate. Before further critical experiments are reviewed, some theoretical questions and consequences call for consideration.

## 4. Consequences and Questions

What conclusions can we draw? First, the evidence reported above is more than enough to eliminate any short-circuiting theory. The two cases just described deprive such explanations of any vestige of plausibility. If electrical currents behaved that way, computers would act even worse than they do. Nevertheless, fondness for reducing psychological to electrical phenomena fades slowly. As Kolers writes (*AMP*, 180): "The short-circuit theory has been refuted more times than any other in perceptual psychology yet it must capture a quality that many investigators find attractive, for it has lingered on". No doubt some version of it will survive until sunset.

Second, attempted accounts in terms of eye-motion, offered by many psychologists, fail quite as dismally (*AMP*, 72 *ff*). In the cases discussed just above, the eyes—to generate the different motions of the leftmost circle of the first group and the remaining three—would have to move at different speeds and cross in the middle! Moreover, in the second of the two cases, one eye would have to be performing unimaginable other acrobatics at the same time to transform the leftmost circle into a square as it moves. Any eyes that move that way would be more worth watching than the figures. Equally telling is another case (*AMP*, 77), where the displays flashed are: first, the center circle of Figure 2; and second, all four circles lying in different directions from it. The center circle splits into four that proceed

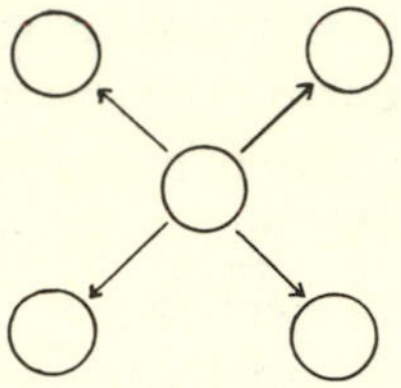

**Figure 2**

severally and simultaneously to the four different corners. Do both eyes move in all four directions at once? Or do they move separately, each in two different directions?

Ridiculing such theories is easier than finding a satisfactory one. A cognitive approach looks more promising. The visual system drives toward uniformity and continuity, constrained by its anatomy and physiology, and influenced by what it has seen and done before, but improvising along the way. This falls far short of a theory accounting in particular for the varied results of these experiments. Even rather cautious generalizations that might serve as first steps toward broader principles frequently fail. For example, in some cases a figure in the display first flashed will move and transform into the *nearest* figure in the second; in other cases, it will move without changing into the nearest figure *of its own shape*, ignoring a nearer figure of different shape (*AMP*, 100–102). Kolers concludes: "No theory of illusory motion has yet been proposed that accommodates more than a few observations" (*AMP*, 181). I suspect that the visual system, while having fun making a world to suit itself, takes incidental glee in frustrating our search for a theory.

More may be said, though, on a couple of theoretical questions raised earlier. First, are apparent-motion perception and real-motion perception substantially the same? The presumption in favor of an affirmative answer is so strong that according to Kolers, "Gibson once remarked that it was 'unfortunate' that a distinction had been drawn between veridical and illusory motions" (*AMP*, 175). We know that in ordinary reading, for example, we pick up fragmentary clues from the text and supplement them copiously; and there seems little reason to suppose that perception of real motion is, in contrast, by continuous tracking. Furthermore, where other changes occur along with motion, constant monitoring of all seems highly improbable. In that the perception of real and of apparent motion both proceed by supplementation from sparse cues, they are indeed alike. Nevertheless, they are also very unlike. In the first place, where real motion deviates from the usual path of apparent motion, the deviation is usually noticed. Thus real-motion perception, unlike apparent-motion perception, cannot be entirely a matter of supplementation between extremes; somehow without continual monitoring we are nevertheless alert for significant cue-selection. Kolers relies instead on two other arguments (*AMP*, 35 *ff*, 174 *ff*). The first is that a subject can learn to tell rather reliably whether he perceived real or apparent motion. Seeing a spot as moving when it does not has a discernibly different quality from seeing a spot actually moving. But perhaps even more conclusive is Kolers' experimental determination that while real motion along crossing paths may be readily perceived, paths of apparent motion never cross. For example (*AMP*, 77), if the top row of Figure 3

**Figure 3**

is flashed first, then the bottom row a little below it, each of the two component figures in the top row moves straight down and transforms into the different shape below it; the circle and the square never move diagonally down to the figures of their own shape below. Real-motion perception and apparent-motion perception, though alike in important ways, are still often very different. But the conjecture that the difference might be explained in terms of activation versus nonactivation of the 'motion-detectors' has been discredited by experimental demonstration that the frog's eye reacts in the same way to successive discrete stimulation as to continuous motion.[7]

The second question asks how supplementation can start off in the right way before the second flash occurs. How does the visual system know in advance whether to go right or left or up or down, to start transforming a square into a circle or a triangle? A plausible explanation, to my mind, is that apparent motion or change, though seen as running from the first to the second flash, is constructed only as or after the second flash occurs. Whether perception of the first flash is thought to be delayed or preserved or remembered, I call this the retrospective construction theory—the theory that the construction perceived as occurring between the two flashes is accomplished not earlier than the second. If this seems a complex and even somewhat fanciful explanation, it strikes me as quite in character with the complex and remarkable phenomena we have been encountering. Furthermore, I think that much the same sort of explanation is indicated for the dream that leads to an eventual actual noise that wakens the dreamer. But, perhaps less ready than I to attribute a certain oddball ingenuity to the visual

---

[7] See the discussion by Kolers (*AMP*, 169) of relevant work by several investigators, e.g. "Neurophysiology of the Anuran Visual System" by O.-J. Grüsser and Ursula Grüsser-Cornhels, *Frog Neurobiology: A Handbook*. R. Llinas and W. Fecht, eds. (Springer, 1976), pp. 297–385.

system, Kolers in his book rejects the retrospective construction theory for apparent motion and change, insisting that the "construction is carried out in real time" (*AMP*, 184);[8] and he suggests that the direction of supplementation is determined by anticipation induced by practice (*AMP*, 196). Since an observer usually does not perceive apparent motion very well until after a few practice runs, perhaps such practice provides the needed guidance.

I remained unconvinced by this explanation; and Kolers told me some time after the book was published that he felt less adamantly opposed to a retrospective construction theory. To settle the question, we badly needed some easily conceived experimentation. For example, in the practice runs, let the dot in the first flashes always be centered in the field, and the dot in the second flashes lie at random in various directions from the center. If on postpractice trials apparent motion is readily and clearly perceived, then the success of supplementation in finding its way cannot be attributed to practice. Only very recently have such experiments, carried out at the University of Oregon,[9] conclusively disposed of the practice hypothesis. That

---

[8] I may have oversimplified here; perhaps the only difference lies in what Kolers and I count as a retrospective construction theory. Kolers' argument in outline runs: since perceiving a stimulus takes up to one-third of a second while the interval between flashes is around a tenth of that, the second flash occurs long before perception of the first flash; the process of constructing the apparent motion may, as the process of perceiving the flashes must, begin before perception of the flashes is achieved; thus the supplementation may be accomplished along with perception of the flashes so that no retrospective construction is involved. However, the process of supplementation can hardly start before the second flash *occurs*; yet in perceptual ordering the apparent motion lies between and connects the two flashes. The initiating sequence, $flash_1$-$flash_2$-supplement, is altered as perceived to $flash_1$-supplement-$flash_2$. Such perceptual reordering I count as retrospective construction.

[9] See "Position Uncertainty and the Perception of Apparent Movement" by J. Beck, Ann Elsner, C. Silverstein in *Perception and Psychophysics*, Vol. 21 (1977), pp. 33–38.

seems to leave us a choice between a retrospective construction theory and a belief in clairvoyance.

Kolers' searching and significant book, as we have seen, poses many puzzles; but none of these is *the* puzzle about perception referred to in the title of this chapter.

## 5. Color

During the work reported in Koler's book, I often urged him to look into another question: What happens when the successively flashed displays differ in color? Kolers agreed on the interest of the matter but had no opportunity to design and construct the required apparatus for such experiments while the work on change in position, shape, and size was in progress. Thus in his book Kolers refers only to the somewhat sketchy work of others on this question, e.g., "Squires confirmed Wertheimer's finding that differences in color were resolved smoothly by the visual system" (*AMP*, 43). But apparently no one had investigated the *route* of such resolution. This question especially interested me for the following reason: If we could find out whether the route of change from, say, red to green passes through median gray or through the spectral hues orange and yellow or bypasses all of these, we might have a new and experimental basis for confirming or recasting the standard ordering of colors.[10] That is, we might take the path thus followed between each two colors as a straight line—the shortest distance —between the two, and go on to reconstruct what might turn

---

[10] The standard ordering consists of a solid sphere or double pyramid with the hues in spectral sequence around the equator, intensity varying with latitude, and purity with nearness to the surface. This has the important virtue of being standard but no firm claim to being the unique or primary perceptual ordering of colors. It is commonly presupposed but rarely subjected to throughgoing theoretic and experimental investigation. See further *SA*, pp. 268–276.

out to be either the familiar color-solid or something quite different but would be a definitive mapping of one important sort of color similarity.

After finishing his book, Kolers with an associate, von Grunau, did carry out the proposed experiments on color change and reported the results in two papers.[11] In these experiments, the displays successively flashed were of different colors—sometimes contrasting, even complementary, colors such as red and green, sometimes colors more nearly alike such as red and deep pink. Sometimes the figures flashed were the same in size and shape; sometimes the first might be, say, a small red square while the second was a large green (or pink) circle.

As expected, the color differences do not at all interfere with smooth apparent transition in place, size, or shape. But what course does the transition in color take? Straight through the color solid? On the surface? Or on some other path? Over some years, Kolers himself and a variety of other psychologists, as well as nonpsychologists like the present writer, made conjectures. What is yours? None of us came anywhere near guessing right—and neither did you! Common sense, which surely tells us, in the light of the experiments on apparent change in other respects, that the color change will proceed smoothly along some path or other, has here tricked us even worse than usual. The actual result of the experiment is shocking. Flash a small red square and then a large green (or pink) circle, within the specified time and distance limitations, and we see the square, while smoothly moving and transforming and growing into the circle, *remaining red until about midcourse and then abruptly changing to green (or pink)*.

---

[11] See *Science*, Vol. 187 (1975), pp. 757–759, and *Vision Research*, Vol. 16 (1976), pp. 329–335.

This strikes me as one of the most dramatically unexpected results in the history of experimental psychology. And here we do come to the puzzle about perception referred to in my title.

## 6. The Puzzle

How is it that color transition not only works quite differently from transition in place or size or shape but stubbornly so? Even when accompanied (and one would suppose influenced) by smooth change in these other respects, the color jumps. Abundant bridging still occurs; each of the intervening places along a path between the two flashes is filled in, but with one of the flashed colors rather than with successive intermediate colors.

Perhaps the first thought is that since after all color is not place or shape or size, the presumption that apparent color change should parallel change in these other respects is unfounded anyway. But without some explanation of how a specific peculiarity of color can account for the abrupt shift, this helps very little; for place and shape and size also differ from each other in important ways[12] and yet smooth transition occurs in all these respects.

Let us look at three interrelated features of ordinary 'real' perceptual change[13] in spatio-temporal properties, quite apart from the special phenomena we have been considering.

First, smooth perceptual change in shape and size and position of an object when distance and angle of view vary pervades everyday experience. As I watch a cubical object turn, its visual shape gradually transforms. As it moves toward or away from

---

[12] See, for example, SA, pp. 53 ff, 199, 260 ff.

[13] That is, perceptual change concomitant with change in stimulus presented. This does not always imply correlative physical change in the object observed. For example, as I walk around a pyramid the perceptual shape and the stimulus presented vary concomitantly while the physical shape remains constant.

me it grows or shrinks visually. And as it moves left or right or up or down it may traverse the visual field.

Second, such perceptual change is often produced by moving ourselves or our eyes or by manipulating the object. Thus not only does such change occur again and again in the normal course of events, but we may in many cases bring it about and run through it at will. It becomes thoroughly learned by both observation and practice.

Third, unfilled spatio-temporal gaps are seldom encompassed within an object. We strive mightily and resourcefully, consciously and automatically, to supply whatever is required to join separate pieces into one object or pseudo-object, as in the familiar cases of Figure 4.

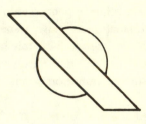 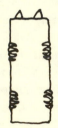

**Figure 4**

But unless we somehow manage—perceptually or conceptually or conjecturally—to fill in between two separated entities or events, we resist combining them into one thing; and where we observe abrupt change in shape or size without change in location, we characteristically read it as replacement rather than transformation of an object. Connectivity is a standard, if not unexceptionable, requirement for objective unity.

Now compare on all these scores our experience with color. First, gradual color change is by no means so predominant as gradual spatio-temporal change. Smooth transition between shades of color does occur in the waxing or waning light of dawn or dusk or dimmer-switch. On the other hand, smooth transition between contrasting hues is rare, while abrupt changes occur profusely whenever our eyes move across the patchworks of color that almost always confront us.

Second, we cannot easily *produce* gradual transition between different colors as we can between different positions or shapes or sizes. Nothing comparable to simple voluntary movement of eyes or body, without auxiliary apparatus, will change color smoothly or in any regular and predictable way.

Third, gaps in color, unlike spatio-temporal gaps, offer no obstacle to object unity. Most ordinary things, from people to houses to neckties, contain within them sharply bounded regions of contrasting colors; and colors intervening between the black and red of a checkerboard need not be supplied for us to take the board as a single object. Normally, all that is required is contrast at the outer edges with the background.[14] Furthermore, quick changes of color under flashing lights we take as changes in perceived color of the same object rather than as replacement by an object of different color. And an object does not lose its identity as it passes through dappled sun and shade. [15]

---

[14] Sometimes the perceptual system even supplies missing parts of contours. See for example interesting recent discussions by John Kennedy in "Attention, Brightness, and the Constructive Eye", *Vision and Artifact*, M. Henle, ed. (Springer, 1976), pp. 33–47, and by Gaetano Kanizsa in "Contours without Gradients or Cognitive Contours?", *Italian Journal of Psychology*, Vol. 1 (1974) pp. 93–113.

[15] Since color leaps are compatible with identity of object or figure, we may ask why, when a black square is twice flashed against white without change in place or size or shape, we see it as lasting through the· whole period rather than as black-then-white-then-black? The answer is obvious: continuation of the black (or other color different from white) is required for continuity of the figure. A white stage would lose the contour so that the flashes of the black square would be seen as separate events. Color gaps, ordinarily quite acceptable, may be filled in for the sake of preserving contour and continuity.

In sum, smooth resolution of spatio-temporal disparities, unlike smooth resolution of color-contrasts, is a commonplace in ordinary experience, can often be effected voluntarily and repeatedly, and is demanded for organization into most objects we operate with in our everyday world. That goes a good way, I think, toward explaining why in the Kolers experiments the perceptual system—true to its experience, its practice, and its role—handles spatio-temporal and color disparities in different ways.

Can we leave it at that? Does this cover everything pertinent to the startling results of the color experiments? On the contrary, I think we have missed the most central and conspicious consideration of all: *that virtually every clear case of visual motion perception depends upon abrupt shift in color.*

Consider a solid black square moving at moderate speed from left to right against a white background. At each moment, the left edge of the black flicks to white, merging with the background, while the white bordering the right edge of the black flicks to black, becoming part of the square. There are no perceptible spatio-temporal gaps between immediately successive changes at each edge—they make up a continuous process. But the component color changes themselves are leaps between black and white—there is no passing through intermediate grays. This constitutes the motion perception. Only so is continuity of contour preserved; the black square remains throughout the same black square (or in other cases transforms smoothly in size or shape) contrasting all along the perimeter with the white background. More generally, whatever the size and shape and color of the figure or object viewed, such continuous leaping between the different colors at the edges is part and parcel of real-motion perception; and so also for apparent-motion perception insofar as it approximates real-motion perception.

With the visual system taking such leaps in stride, with their indispensability for motion-perception, with object-identity dependent not upon smooth color transition but upon contrast with the background at the contour, the color-jumps in the Kolers experiments seem so inevitable as to leave us wondering how we let a false analogy trick us into expecting anything different.

So our puzzle about perception evaporates; but the fascinating facts of apparent change and the problem of arriving at a general explanation remain. The puzzle, while its history seems to me engaging and humiliating, is of less concern for our purposes than are the phenomena themselves. Notice in retrospect, that these have been studied, experimented upon, debated, as objectively as facts of physics. The task of finding the facts does not become arbitrary or pointless when the facts are of 'apparent' rather than of 'real' or of physical motion. "Apparent" and "real" here are insidiously prejudicial labels for facts of different kinds. Just as the motion of a dot across a screen is sometimes 'not there' in stimulus or object, so the separate static flashes are sometimes 'not there' in perception. What we have been looking at are some striking examples of how perception makes its facts.[16] This, together with the discussion in Chapters II–IV of some other particular means and kinds of worldmaking, brings us back to the more general study begun in Chapter I.

---

[16] Other striking examples may be found in the perceptual construction of contours (see note 14 above) and also of color, which according to Edwin H. Land depends not upon particular wavelength but rather upon 'sudden changes in energy'; (see his paper, "Our polar partnership with the world around us", *Harvard Magazine*, Vol. 80 (1978) pp. 23–26, and "The Retinex Theory of Color Vision" in *Scientific American*, Vol. 237 (1977), pp. 108–128.) For still further experiments on motion perception, see E. Sigman and I. Rock "Stroboscopic Movement based on Perceptual Intelligence", *Perception*, Vol. 3 (1974), pp. 9–28.

# VI

# The Fabrication of Facts

## 1. Actuality and Artifice

The chapter before began with the rather reproachful question "Can't you see what's before you?", and arrived at the illuminating answer "That depends...". One thing it depends on is the answer to another question: "Well, what's before me?" That's the question I begin with here, and I must confess that the answer to this, too, is "That depends...", and one thing it depends on heavily is the answer to still another question: "What do you make of it?"

My title, "The Fabrication of Facts", has the virtue not only of indicating pretty clearly what I am going to discuss but also of irritating those fundamentalists who know very well that facts are found not made, that facts constitute the one and only real world, and that knowledge consists of believing the facts. These articles of faith so firmly possess most of us, they so bind and blind us, that "fabrication of fact" has a paradoxical sound. "Fabrication" has become a synonym for "falsehood" or "fiction" as contrasted with "truth" or "fact". Of course, we must distinguish falsehood and fiction from truth and fact; but we cannot, I am sure, do it on the ground that fiction is fabricated and fact found.

Look back a moment at the case of so-called apparent motion. The experimental results I have summarized are not universal; they are merely typical. Not only do different observers perceive motion differently, but some cannot see apparent motion at all. Those who are thus unable to see what they know is not there are classed as naive realists by Kolers, who reports a disproportionately high percentage of them among engineers and physicians (*AMP*, 160).

Yet if an observer reports that he sees two distinct flashes, even at distances and intervals so short that most observers see one moving spot, perhaps he means that he sees the two as we might say we see a swarm of molecules when we look at a chair, or as we do say we see a round table top even when we look at it from an oblique angle. Since an observer can become adept at distinguishing apparent from real motion, he may take the appearance of motion as a sign that there are two flashes, as we take the oval appearance of the table top as a sign that it is round; and in both cases the signs may be or become so transparent that we look through them to physical events and objects. When the observer visually determines that what is before him is what we agree is before him, we can hardly charge him with an error in visual perception. Shall we say, rather, that he misunderstands the instruction, which is presumably just to tell what he sees? Then how, without prejudicing the outcome, can we so reframe that instruction as to prevent such a 'misunderstanding'? Asking him to make no use of prior experience and to avoid all conceptualization will obviously leave him speechless; for to talk at all he must use words.

The best we can do is to specify the sort of terms, the vocabulary, he is to use, telling him to describe what he sees in perceptual or phenomenal rather than physical terms. Whether or not this yields different responses, it casts an entirely different light on what is happening. That the instruments to be used in fashioning the facts must be specified makes pointless any identification of the physical with the real and of the perceptual with the merely apparent. The perceptual is no more a rather distorted version of the physical facts than the physical is a highly artificial version of the perceptual facts. If we are tempted to say that 'both are versions of the same facts', this must no more be taken to imply that there are independent facts of which both are versions than likeness of meaning between two terms implies that there are some entities called meanings. "Fact" like "meaning" is a syncategorematic term; for facts, after all, are obviously factitious.

The point is classically illustrated, again, by variant versions of physical motion. Did the sun set a while ago or did the earth rise? Does the sun go around the earth or the earth go around the sun? Nowadays, we nonchalantly deal with what was once a life-and-death issue by saying that the answer depends on the framework. But here again, if we say that the geocentric and heliocentric systems are different versions of 'the same facts', we must ask not what these facts are but rather how such phrases as "versions of the same facts" or "descriptions of the same world" are to be understood. This varies from case to case; here, the geocentric and the heliocentric versions, while speaking of the same particular objects—the sun, moon, and planets—attribute very different motions to these objects. Still, we may say the two versions deal with the same facts if we mean by this that they not only speak of the same objects but are also routinely translatable each into the other. As meanings vanish in favor of certain relationships among terms, so facts vanish in favor of certain relationships among versions. In the present case, the relationship is comparatively obvious; sometimes it is much more elusive. For instance, the physical and perceptual versions of motion we were talking about do not evidently deal with all the same objects, and the relationship if any that constitutes license for saying that the two versions describe the same facts or the same world is no ready intertranslatability.

The physical and perceptual world-versions mentioned are

but two of the vast variety in the several sciences, in the arts, in perception, and in daily discourse. Worlds are made by making such versions with words, numerals, pictures, sounds, or other symbols of any kind in any medium; and the comparative study of these versions and visions and of their making is what I call a critique of worldmaking. I began such a study in Chapter I, and I shall now have to summarize and clarify some points in that chapter very briefly before going on to the further problems that are the main concern of the present chapter.

## 2. Means and Matter

What I have said so far plainly points to a radical relativism; but severe restraints are imposed. Willingness to accept countless alternative true or right world-versions does not mean that everything goes, that tall stories are as good as short ones, that truths are no longer distinguished from falsehoods, but only that truth must be otherwise conceived than as correspondence with a ready-made world. Though we make worlds by making versions, we no more make a world by putting symbols together at random than a carpenter makes a chair by putting pieces of wood together at random. The multiple worlds I countenance are just the actual worlds made by and answering to true or right versions. Worlds possible or impossible supposedly answering to false versions have no place in my philosophy.

Just what worlds are to be recognized as actual is quite another question. Although some aspects of a philosophical position have a bearing, even what seem severely restrictive views may recognize countless versions as equally right. For example, I am sometimes asked how my relativism can be reconciled with my nominalism. The answer is easy. Although a nominalistic system speaks only of individuals, banning all talk of classes, it may take anything whatever as an individual; that is, the nominalistic prohibition is against the profligate propagation of entities out of any chosen basis of individuals, but leaves the choice of that basis quite free. Nominalism of itself thus authorizes an abundance of alternative versions based on physical particles or phenomenal elements or ordinary things or whatever else one is willing to take as individuals.[1] Nothing here prevents any given nominalist from preferring on other grounds some among the systems thus recognized as legitimate. In contrast, the typical physicalism, for example, while prodigal in the platonistic instruments it supplies for endless generation of entities, admits of only one correct (even if yet unidentified) basis.

Thus while the physicalist's doctrine "no difference without a physical difference" and the nominalist's doctrine "no difference without a difference of individuals" sound alike, they differ notably in this respect.[2]

All the same, in this general discussion of worldmaking I do not impose nominalistic restrictions, for I want to allow for some difference of opinion as to what actual worlds there are.[3] That falls far short of countenancing merely possible worlds. The platonist and I may disagree about what makes an actual world while we agree in rejecting all else. We may disagree in what we take to be true while we agree that nothing answers to what we take to be false.

---

[1] See *SA*, pp. 26–28; *PP*, pp. 157–161.

[2] And in others, especially in that the nominalist's doctrine requires constructional interpretation of every difference in terms of differences between individuals, while the physicalist's doctrine is less explicit, often requiring only some unspecified or at best causal connection between physical and other differences.

[3] In the same spirit, although *SA* is committed to nominalism, its criterion for constructional definitions and its measurement of simplicity were, for comparative purposes, made broad enough to apply to platonistic systems as well. On the other hand, neither there nor here is any allowance made for departures from *extensionalism*.

To speak of worlds as made by versions often offends both by its implicit pluralism and by its sabotage of what I have called 'something stolid underneath'. Let me offer what comfort I can. While I stress the multiplicity of right world-versions, I by no means insist that there are many worlds—or indeed any; for as I have already suggested, the question whether two versions are of the same world has as many good answers as there are good interpretations of the words "versions of the same world". The monist can always contend that two versions need only be right to be accounted versions of the same world. The pluralist can always reply by asking what the world is like apart from all versions. Perhaps the best answer is that given by Professor Woody Allen when he writes:[4]

Can we actually 'know' the universe? My God, it's hard enough finding your way around in Chinatown. The point, however, is: Is there anything out there? And why? And must they be so noisy? Finally, there can be no doubt that the one characteristic of 'reality' is that it lacks essence. That is not to say it has no essence, but merely lacks it. (The reality I speak of here is the same one Hobbes described, but a little smaller.)

The message, I take it, is simply this: never mind mind, essence is not essential, and matter doesn't matter. We do better to focus on versions rather than worlds. Of course, we want to distinguish between versions that do and those that do not refer, and to talk about the things and worlds, if any, referred to; but these things and worlds and even the stuff they are made of—matter, anti-matter, mind, energy, or whatnot—are themselves fashioned by and along with the versions. Facts, as Norwood Hanson says, are theory-laden[5]; they are as theory-

---

[4] Woody Allen, "My Philosophy" in *Getting Even* (1966), Chap. 4, Sec. I.

[5] In *Patterns of Discovery*, Cambridge University Press, (1958), Chap. I, and throughout.

laden as we hope our theories are fact-laden. Or in other words, facts are small theories, and true theories are big facts. This does not mean, I must repeat, that right versions can be arrived at casually, or that worlds are built from scratch. We start, on any occasion, with some old version or world that we have on hand and that we are stuck with until we have the determination and skill to remake it into a new one. Some of the felt stubbornness of fact is the grip of habit: our firm foundation is indeed stolid. Worldmaking begins with one version and ends with another.

## 3. Some Ancient Worlds

Let's look for a few moments at some early examples of worldmaking. The pre-Socratics, I have long felt, made almost all the important advances and mistakes in the history of philosphy. Before I consider how their views illustrate topics central to our present discussion, I must give you, much compressed, the inside story of that period of philosophy.

These philosophers, like most of us, started from a world concocted of religion, superstition, suspicion, hope, and bitter and sweet experience. Then Thales, seeking some unity in the jumble, noticed the sun drawing water and heating it to flame, the clouds condensing and falling and drying into earth—and, according to legend, the water at the bottom of a certain well. The solution dawned—indeed, the solution *was* solution: the world is water.

But Anaximander argued, "With earth, air, fire, and water all changing into one another, why pick water? What makes it any different from the other three? We have to find something neutral that all are made from." So he invented the Boundless, thus in one stroke inflicting upon philosophy two of its greatest burdens: infinity and substance.

Empedocles ruled the Boundless out-of-bounds. If there is no choice among the elements, we must take all four; what counts is how they are mixed. He saw that the real secret of the universe is confusion.

When Heraclitus asked for action, Parmenides responded with a stop sign, reducing philosophy to the formula "It is", meaning of course "It is not", or to make a short story long, "Look at the mess we have got ourselves into!"

Democritus, though, deftly rescued us. He replaced "It is" by "They are". The point is that if you slice things fine enough everything will be the same. All particles are alike; the way they are put together makes water or air or fire or earth—or whatever. Quality is supplanted by quantity and structure.

One issue between Thales and his successors reverberates all through philosophical history. Thales reduced all four elements to water; Anaximander and Empedocles objected that the four could as well be reduced to any of the other three. So far, both sides are equally right. Thales' aquacentric system is no better justified as against its three alternatives than a geocentric description of the solar system is justified as against its obvious alternatives. But Thales' critics went wrong in supposing that since none of the alternative systems is exclusively right, all are wrong. That we can do without any one of them does not mean that we can do without all, but only that we have a choice. The implicit ground for rejecting Thales' theory was that features distinguishing alternative systems cannot reflect reality as it is. Thus Empedocles insisted that any ordering among the four elements is an arbitrary imposition on reality. What he overlooked is that any organizing into elements is no less an imposition, and that if we prohibit all such impositions we end with nothing. Anaximander had grasped, and indeed embraced, this consequence and treated the four elements as derivative from a neutral and nugatory Boundless. The logical Parmenides concluded that if only something completely neutral can be common to the worlds of all alternative versions, only *that* is real and all else is mere illusion; but even he organized that reality in a special way: the It that is is One. Democritus, thus invited, promptly organized it differently, breaking it into small pieces—and off we were again.

Under much of this controversy concerning what can be reduced to what, lies the recurrent question what constitutes reduction. That water changes into the other elements does not, Anaximander objected, make them merely water; and neither, Empedocles in effect retorted, does construing the elements as made of a neutral substance make them merely neutral substance. Here are precursors of current campaigns, by friends and enemies of physical objects or phenomena or concreta or qualities or mind or matter, against or for dispensing with any of these in favor of others. Such campaigns characteristically spring from misunderstanding of the requirements upon and the significance of what is as much construction as reduction.

## 4. Reduction and Construction

Debates concerning criteria for constructional definitions have often centered upon whether intensional or only extensional agreement is required between definiens and definiendum. The demand for absolute synonymy was grounded in the conviction that the definiens must be an explanation of the meaning of the definiendum. Trouble with the notion of meanings and even with the idea of exact sameness of meaning raised the question whether extensional identity might do, but this in turn proved too tight, for often multiple alternative definientia that are not coextensive are obviously equally admissible. For example, a point in a plane may be defined either as a certain pair of intersecting lines or as a quite different pair or as a nest of regions, etc.; but the definientia having these disjoint extensions surely cannot all be co-extensive with the definiendum.

Such considerations point to a criterion framed in terms of an extensional isomorphism that requires preservation of structure rather than of extension. Since a structure may be common to many different extensions; this allows for legitimate alternative definientia. The isomorphism in question is global, required to obtain between the whole set of definientia of a system and the whole set of their definienda, but is not symmetric: normally, as in the mentioned definitions of points, a definiens articulates its extension more fully than does the definiendum, and thus performs an analysis and introduces means for systematic integration.[6]

So conceived, definition of points in terms of lines or sets makes no claim that points are merely lines or sets; and derivation of the other elements from water makes no claim that they are merely water. Insofar as the definitions or derivations are successful, they organize the points and lines, or the four elements, into a system. That there are alternative systems discredits none of them; for there is no alternative but blankness to alternative systems, to organization of one kind or another. To his successors who complained that Thales was introducing artificial order and priorities, he might well have rejoined that that is what science and philosophy do, and that complete elimination of the so-called artificial would leave us empty-minded and empty-handed.[7] With the reconception of the nature and significance of reduction or construction or derivation or systematization we give up our futile search for the aboriginal world, and come to recognize that systems and other versions

---

[6] See further SA: I. In some circumstances, criteria even looser than extensional isomorphism may be appropriate.

[7] See further VII:2 below on convention and content.

are as productive as reproductive.

In the foregoing history of thought from Thales to Allen, several of the processes of worldmaking—or relation between worlds—that I discussed in Chapter I have been illustrated: *ordering*, in the derivation of all four elements from one; *supplementation*, in the introduction of the Boundless; *deletion*, in the elimination of everything else; and *division*, in the shattering of the One into atoms. Supplementation and deletion are also dramatically illustrated in the relation between the world of physics and a familiar perceptual world. Among other processes or relationships mentioned were *composition*, as when events are combined into an enduring object; *deformation*, as when rough curves are smoothed out; and *weighting* or emphasis. The last of these, less often noted and less well understood, yet especially important for what follows, needs some further attention here.

Worldmaking sometimes, without adding or dropping entities, alters emphasis; and a difference between two versions that consists primarily or even solely in their relative weighting of the same entities may be striking and consequential. For one notable example, consider the differences in what may be taken by two versions to be natural or relevant kinds—that is, to be the kinds important for description or investigation or induction. Our habitual projection of "green" and "blue" does not deny that "grue" and "bleen" name classes, but treats these classes as trivial.[8] To reverse this—to project "grue" and "bleen" rather than "green" and "blue"—would be to make, and live in, a different world. A second example of the effect of weighting appears in the difference between two histories of the Renaissance: one that, without excluding the battles, stresses the arts; and another that, without excluding the arts, stresses the

---

[8] Such loose platonistic talk should be taken as vernacular for a nominalistic formulation in terms of predicates.

battles (II:2). This difference in style is a difference in weighting that gives us two different Renaissance worlds.

## 5. Fact from Fiction

With all this variety, attention usually focuses on versions that are literal, denotational, and verbal. While that covers some—though I think far from all—scientific and quasi-scientific worldmaking, it leaves out perceptual and pictorial versions and all figurative and exemplificational means and all nonverbal media. The worlds of fiction, poetry, painting, music, dance, and the other arts are built largely by such nonliteral devices as metaphor, by such nondenotational means as exemplification and expression, and often by use of pictures or sounds or gestures or other symbols of nonlinguistic systems. Such worldmaking and such versions are my primary concern here; for a major thesis of this book is that the arts must be taken no less seriously than the sciences as modes of discovery, creation, and enlargement of knowledge in the broad sense of advancement of the understanding, and thus that the philosophy of art should be conceived as an integral part of metaphysics and epistemology.

Consider, first, versions that are visions, depictions rather than descriptions. On the syntactic side, pictures differ radically from words—pictures are not comprised of items from an alphabet, are not identified across a variety of hands and fonts, do not combine with other pictures or with words to make sentences. But pictures and terms alike denote—apply as labels—to whatever they represent or name or describe.[9] Names and such pictures as individual and group portraits denote uniquely,

---

[9] On the general matter of the difference between linguistic and pictorial symbol systems, see *LA*, esp. pp. 41–43, 225–227. For further discussion of denotation by pictures, see my comments on a paper by Monroe Beardsley, in *Erkenntnis* Vol. 12 (1978), pp. 169–70.

while predicates and such pictures as those in an ornithologist's guide denote generally. Thus pictures may make and present facts and participate in worldmaking in much the same way as do terms. Indeed, our everyday so-called picture of the world is the joint product of description and depiction. Yet I must repeat that I am here subscribing neither to any picture theory of language nor to any language theory of pictures; for pictures belong to nonlinguistic, and terms to nonpictorial, symbol systems.

Some depictions and descriptions, though, do not literally denote anything. Painted or written portrayals of Don Quixote, for example, do not denote Don Quixote—who is simply not there to be denoted. Works of fiction in literature and their counterparts in other arts obviously play a prominent role in worldmaking; our worlds are no more a heritage from scientists, biographers, and historians than from novelists, playwrights, and painters. But how can versions of nothing thus participate in the making of actual worlds? The inevitable proposal to supply fictive entities and possible worlds as denotata will not, even for those who can swallow it, help with this question. Yet the answer, once sought, comes rather readily.

"Don Quixote", taken literally, applies to no one, but taken figuratively, applies to many of us—for example, to me in my tilts with the windmills of current linguistics. To many others the term applies neither literally nor metaphorically. Literal falsity or inapplicability is entirely compatible with, but of course no guarantee of, metaphorical truth; and the line between metaphorical truth and metaphorical falsity intersects, but is no more arbitrary than, the line between literal truth and literal falsity. Whether a person is a Don Quixote (i.e., quixotic) or a Don Juan is as genuine a question as whether a person is paranoid or schizophrenic, and rather easier to decide. And application of the fictive term "Don Quixote" to actual people, like the metaphorical application of the nonfictive term "Napoleon" to other generals and like the literal application of some newly invented term such as "vitamin" or "radioactive" to materials, effects a reorganization of our familiar world by picking out and underlining as a relevant kind a category that cuts across well-worn ruts. Metaphor is no mere decorative rhetorical device but a way we make our terms do multiple moonlighting service.[10]

Fiction, then, whether written or painted or acted, applies truly neither to nothing nor to diaphanous possible worlds but, albeit metaphorically, to actual worlds. Somewhat as I have argued elsewhere that the merely possible[11]—so far as admissible at all—lies within the actual, so we might say here again, in a different context, that the so-called possible worlds of fiction lie within actual worlds. Fiction operates in actual worlds in much the same way as nonfiction. Cervantes and Bosch and Goya, no less than Boswell and Newton and Darwin, take and

[10] On metaphorical truth, see further *LA*, pp. 68-70. On meaning-relationships between different fictive terms like "Don Quixote" and "Don Juan", see *PP*, pp. 221-238, and Israel Scheffler's important paper "Ambiguity: an Inscriptional Approach" in *Logic and Art*, R. Rudner and I. Scheffler, eds. (Bobbs-Merrill, 1972), pp. 251-272. Notice that since "Don Quixote" and "Don Juan" have the same (null) literal extension, their metaphorical sorting of people cannot reflect any literal sorting. How then can the metaphorical behavior of these terms be subsumed under the general theory of metaphor? In two closely interrelated ways. The metaphorical sorting may reflect: (1) difference in literal extension between parallel compounds of the two terms—for example, "Don-Quixote-term (or picture)" and "Don-Juan-term (or picture)" have different literal extensions; or (2) difference in the terms that denote, and may be exemplified by, the two terms—for example, "Don Juan" is an inveterate-seducer-term while "Don Quixote" is not. In sum, "Don Quixote" and "Don Juan" are denoted by different terms (e.g., "Don-Quixote-term" and "Don-Juan-term") that also denote other different terms (e.g., "zany jouster" and "inveterate seducer") that in turn denote different people. If this is somewhat complicated, the component steps are all simple; and any trafficking with fictive entities is avoided.

[11] *FFF*, pp. 49-58. I am by no means here letting down the bars to admit merely possible worlds, but only suggesting that some talk that is ostensibly 'about possible things' can be usefully reinterpreted as talk about actual things.

unmake and remake and retake familiar worlds, recasting them in remarkable and sometimes recondite but eventually recognizable—that is *re-cognizable*—ways.

But what of purely abstract paintings and other works that have no subject, that do not apply to anything literally or metaphorically, that even the most permissive philosophers would hardly regard as depicting any world, possible or actual? Such works, unlike Don Quixote portraits or centaur pictures, are not literal labels on empty jars or fanciful labels on full ones; they are not labels at all. Are they, then, to be cherished in and for themselves only, as the pure-in-spirit uncontaminated by contact with any world? Of course not; our worlds are no less powerfully informed by the patterns and feelings of abstract works than by a literal Chardin still-life or an allegorical "Birth of Venus". After we spend an hour or so at one or another exhibition of abstract painting, everything tends to square off into geometric patches or swirl in circles or weave into textural arabesques, to sharpen into black and white or vibrate with new color consonances and dissonances. Yet how can what does not either literally or figuratively depict or describe or declare or denote or otherwise apply to anything whatever so transform our well-worn worlds?

We have seen earlier that what does not denote may still *refer* by exemplification or expression, and that nondescriptive, nonrepresentational works nevertheless function as symbols for features they possess either literally or metaphorically. Serving as samples of, and thereby focussing attention upon, certain— often upon unnoticed or neglected—shared or shareable forms, colors, feelings, such works induce reorganization of our accustomed world in accordance with these features, thus dividing and combining erstwhile relevant kinds, adding and subtracting, effecting new discriminations and integrations, reordering priorities. Indeed, symbols may work through exemplification and expression as well as through denotation in any or all of the various already mentioned ways of worldmaking.

Music obviously works in like ways upon the auditory realm, but it also participates in producing whatever conglomerate linguistic and nonlinguistic visual version we tend to take at a given moment as our 'picture of the world'. For the forms and feelings of music are by no means all confined to sound; many patterns and emotions, shapes, contrasts, rhymes, and rhythms are common to the auditory and the visual and often to the tactual and the kinesthetic as well. A poem, a painting, and a piano sonata may literally and metaphorically exemplify some of the same features; and any of these works may thus have effects transcending its own medium. In these days of experimentation with the combination of media in the performing arts, nothing is clearer than that music affects seeing, that pictures affect hearing, that both affect and are affected by the movement of dance. They all interpenetrate in making a world.

Exemplification and expression are of course functions not of abstract works exclusively but also of many descriptive and representational works, fictional and nonfictional. What a portrait or a novel exemplifies or expresses often reorganizes a world more drastically than does what the work literally or figuratively says or depicts; and sometimes the subject serves merely as a vehicle for what is exemplified or expressed. But whether alone or in combination, the several modes and means of symbolization are powerful instruments. With them, a Japanese haiku or five-line poem by Samuel Menashe can renovate and remodel a world; without them, the moving of mountains by an environmental artist would be futile.

The artist's resources—modes of reference, literal and nonliteral, linguistic and nonlinguistic, denotational and non-denotational, in many media—seem more varied and impressive than the scientist's. But to suppose that science is flatfootedly linguistic, literal, and denotational would be to overlook, for instance, the analog instruments often used, the metaphor involved in measurement when a numerical scheme is applied in a new realm, and the talk in current physics and astronomy of charm and strangeness and black holes. Even if the ultimate product of science, unlike that of art, is a literal, verbal or mathematical, denotational theory, science and art proceed in much the same way with their searching and building.

My outline of the facts concerning the fabrication of facts is of course itself a fabrication; but as I have cautioned more than once, recognition of multiple alternative world-versions betokens no policy of laissez-faire. Standards distinguishing right from wrong versions become, if anything, more rather than less important. But what standards? Not only does countenancing unreconciled alternatives put truth in a different light, but broadening our purview to include versions and visions that make no statements and may even not describe or depict anything requires consideration of standards other than truth. Truth is often inapplicable, is seldom sufficient, and must sometimes give way to competing criteria. These matters I want to discuss in the following chapter.

# VII

# On Rightness of Rendering

## 1. Worlds in Conflict

With multiple and sometimes unreconciled and even unreconcilable theories and descriptions recognized as admissible alternatives, our notions about truth call for some reexamination. And with our view of worldmaking expanded far beyond theories and descriptions, beyond statements, beyond language, beyond denotation even, to include versions and visions metaphorical as well as literal, pictorial and musical as well as verbal, exemplifying and expressing as well as describing and depicting, the distinction between true and false falls far short of marking the general distinction between right and wrong versions. What standard of rightness then, for example, is the counterpart of truth for works without subjects that present worlds by exemplification or expression? I shall have to approach such forbidding questions circumspectly.

In the title of this chapter, both "rendering" and "rightness" are to be taken rather generally. Under "rendering", I include not just what a draftsman does but all the ways of making and presenting worlds—in scientific theories, works of art, and versions of all sorts. I choose the term to counteract any impression that I shall be discussing moral or ethical rightness.[1] Under

---

[1] Any treatment of rightness may, of course, give rise to speculation concerning an application to moral rightness; but I willingly leave that to others. One

"rightness" I include, along with truth, standards of acceptability that sometimes supplement or even compete with truth where it applies, or replace truth for nondeclarative renderings.

Although my main concern here is with these other standards, I must begin with another and closer look at truth. Most of us learned long ago such fundamental principles as that truths never really conflict, that all true versions are true in[2] the only actual world, and that apparent disagreements among truths amount merely to differences in the frameworks or conventions adopted. While most of us also learned a little later to mistrust fundamental principles learned earlier, I am afraid that my remark above about conflicting truths and multiple actual worlds may be passed over as purely rhetorical. They are not; and even at the cost of some repetition, I must make that clearer by a more consecutive account of certain points already often urged throughout these pages. We shall need a sound basis for comparison when we come to the main business of this chapter.

To anyone but an arrant absolutist, alternative ostensibly conflicting versions often present good and equal claims to truth. We can hardly take conflicting statements as true in the same world without admitting all statements whatsoever (since all follow from any contradiction) as true in the same world, and that world itself as impossible. Thus we must either reject one of two ostensibly conflicting versions as false, or take them as true in different worlds, or find if we can another way of reconciling them.

---

point might be pondered, though: in the present context at least, relativity of rightness and the admissibility of conflicting right renderings in no way precludes rigorous standards for distinguishing right from wrong.

[2] I say that a statement is true *in* (or *for*) a given actual world if that statement is true insofar as that world alone is taken into consideration. On the different locutions "true of" and "true about" see my paper with Joseph Ullian, "Truth About Jones", *Journal of Philosophy*, Vol. 74 (1977) pp. 317–338.

In some cases, apparently conflicting truths can be reconciled by clearing away an ambiguity of one sort or another.[3] Sometimes, for example, sentences seem incompatible only because they are elliptical, and when expanded by explicit inclusion of erstwhile implicit restrictions, they plainly speak of different things or different parts of things. Statements affirming that all soldiers are equipped with bows and arrows and that none are so equipped are both true—for soldiers of different eras; the statements that the Parthenon is intact and that it is ruined are both true—for different temporal parts of the building; and the statement that the apple is white and that it is red are both true—for different spatial parts of the apple. Sentences at odds with one another get along better when kept apart. In each of these cases, the two ranges of application combine readily into a recognized kind or object; and the two statements are true in different parts or subclasses of the same world.

But peace cannot always be made so easily. Consider again descriptions of the motion (or nonmotion) of the earth. On the face of it, the two statements

(1) The earth always stands still
(2) The earth dances the role of Petrouchka

conflict since the negate of each follows from the other. And they seem to be about the same earth. Yet each is true—within an appropriate system.[4]

---

[3] On various types of ambiguity, see Israel Scheffler, "Ambiguity: An Inscriptional Approach" in *Logic and Art*, Rudner and Scheffler, eds. (Bobbs-Merrill, 1972), pp. 251–272; and also a forthcoming book by Scheffler.

[4] I am not concerned here with controversies over whether in some absolute sense the earth is still or moves in a particular way. The reader who holds that neither or only one of (1) and (2) is true may substitute his own example; for instance he will perhaps agree that "The earth rotates clockwise" and "The earth rotates counterclockwise" are both true, from different points of view.

Now we shall surely be told that those last four words point the way out: that here again the statements are elliptical, and when expanded by explicit relativization so that they read, for example,

(3) In the Ptolemaic system, the earth stands always still
(4) In a certain Stravinsky-Fokine-like system, the earth dances the role of Petrouchka,

they are seen to be entirely compatible. But this argument works too well. To see why (3) and (4) cannot by any means be accepted as—or even among—fuller formulations of (1) and (2), notice that while at least one of the conflicting statements

(5) The kings of Sparta had two votes
(6) The kings of Sparta had only one vote

is false, both of the following are true:

(7) According to Herodotus, the kings of Sparta had two votes
(8) According to Thucydides, the kings of Sparta had only one vote.

Clearly (7) and (8), unlike (5) and (6), are entirely noncommittal as to how many votes the kings had. Whether someone makes a statement and whether that statement is true are altogether different questions. Similarly (3) and (4), unlike (1) and (2), are entirely noncommittal as to the earth's motion; they do not tell us how or whether the earth moves unless a clause is added to each affirming that what the system in question says is true. But if that is done, then of course (1) and (2) are themselves affirmed and no resolution of the conflict is achieved. The apparently powerful and universal device of relativization to system or version thus misses the mark.

Perhaps, though, we can reconcile sentences like (1) and (2) by relativization to points or frames of reference rather than to systems or versions. A simpler example will be easier to handle here. The equally true conflicting sentences concerning the daily motion[5] of the earth and sun

(9) The earth rotates, while the sun is motionless
(10) The earth is motionless, while the sun revolves around it

might be interpreted as amounting to

(11) The earth rotates relative to the sun
(12) The sun revolves relative to the earth,

which are nonconflicting truths.

What must be noticed, however, is that (11) does not quite say, as (9) does, that the earth rotates; and (12) does not quite say, as (10) does, that the earth is motionless. That an object moves relative to another does not imply either that the first one moves or that the second does not.[6] Indeed, where $f$ is an appropriate formula, (11) and (12) alike amount to the single statement

(13) The spatial relationships between the earth and the sun vary with time according to formula $f$;[7]

and this does not attribute motion or rest to the earth or the sun but is entirely compatible not only with (9) and (10) but also with the statement that the earth rotates for a time and then stops while the sun moves around it. The reconciliation of (9) and (10) is here effected by cancelling out those features respon-

---

[5] I am purposely and harmlessly oversimplifying here by ignoring all other motion such as annual revolution.

[6] The temptation is to replace such a phrase as "relative to the sun" by something like "taking the sun as fixed". But what does that mean? Perhaps something like "representing the sun by a fixed dot on a sheet of paper"; but that is only to say "representing the sun by a dot fixed relative to the sheet of paper", and the original problem recurs.

[7] For the moment I purposely pass over the relativity to observer or framework of distance between objects; but see Section 2 below.

sible for their disagreement; (11), (12), (13) dispense with motion in any sense such that we can ask whether or not or how much a given object moves.

At this juncture we may be inclined to say "Good riddance; such questions are obviously empty anyway". On the other hand, we are severely handicapped if rather than saying whether or how a given object moves, we are restricted to describing changes in relative position. A frame of reference is practically indispensable in most contexts. An astronomer can no more work with a neutral statement like (13) in conducting his observations than we can use a map without locating ourselves on it in finding our way around a city. If there is no difference in what (9) and (10) describe, still there seems to be a significant difference in how they describe it. And so on second thought we are tempted to say that the 'empty' questions are, rather, 'external' as contrasted with 'internal' questions,[8] that they pertain to discourse as contrasted with fact, to convention as contrasted with content. But then we may well have qualms about resting anything on such notoriously dubious dichotomies. For the moment, though, let's leave it at that and consider a different case.

Suppose for now that our universe of discourse is limited to a square segment of a plane, with the two pairs of boundary lines labelled "vertical" and "horizontal". If we assume that there are points, whatever they may be, then the two sentences

(14) Every point is made up of a vertical and a horizontal line
(15) No point is made up of lines or anything else[9]

---

[8] See the controversy between Carnap and Quine in *The Philosophy of Rudolph Carnap*, Schilpp, ed. (La Salle, 1963), pp. 385–406; 915–922.

[9] *Cf. SA*: I. In the present context, I use such informal terms as "made up of", "combination of", "contains", as indeterminate between the terminology of individuals and that of classes.

Of course there are countless alternatives other than (14) and (15) that conflict with both; points may be construed as made up of opposing diagonals, or of any other two or more lines having a common intersection, or construed in various ways in terms of regions.

conflict, but are equally true under appropriate systems. We
know that simple relativization to system, as in (3) and (4), is a
specious way of resolving the conflict. The truth of the
statement in question made by each system must also be affirmed; and if the systems, respectively, say (14) and (15) as they
stand, the conflict remains.

Can we, then, perhaps reconcile (14) and (15) by restricting
their ranges of application? If in our space there are only lines
and combinations of lines then (14) but not (15) may be true,
while if there are only points then (15) but not (14) may be
true. The trouble is, though, that if there are both lines and
points, (14) and (15) still cannot both be true, though neither is
singled out as the false one. If (14) and (15) are alternative truths
they are so within different realms, and these realms cannot be
combined into one where both statements are true.[10] This case
is thus radically different from those where ostensibly conflicting statements about the color of an object or the equipment of
soldiers can be reconciled by confinement of scope to different
parts of the object or to different soldiers; for (14) and (15) cannot easily be construed as applying to different points or different parts of a point. Together they say that every point is,
but that no point is, made up of lines. Although (14) may be
true in our sample space taken as consisting solely of lines, and
(15) true in that space taken as consisting solely of points, still
both cannot be true in that space or any subregion of it taken as

_____

[10] Nor, again, can (14) and the conflicting statement (call it "14a") that points
are made up of opposing diagonals both be true in the realm of all lines and all
combinations thereof. The realms for (14) and (14a) must be differently restricted; for example, that for (14) to lines parallel to the boundaries and that for
(14a) to diagonals. Or all these lines may be admitted for both, but combinations of crossing lines restricted for (14) to vertical-horizontal cases and for (14a)
to opposing diagonals. Incidentally, notice that "realm" is not used here in the
special technical sense given it in LA, p. 72.

consisting of both points and lines. Where we have more comprehensive systems or versions that conflict as do (14) and (15),
their realms are thus less aptly regarded as within one world
than as two different worlds, and even—since the two refuse to
unite peaceably—as worlds in conflict.

## 2. Convention and Content

Since that conclusion may not be widely and warmly
welcomed, let us look for some way of dealing with the conflict
between (14) and (15) without confining them to antagonistic
worlds. Our earlier efforts at reconciliation by relativization to
system were perhaps not so much in the wrong direction as too
simple-minded. Not only must we suppose that the correctness
of the systems in question is tacitly affirmed, but we must
examine more closely what (14) and (15) say as statements
within those systems.

   If, as I have argued before, the criterion for correctness of
such systems is that they set up an overall correlation meeting
certain conditions of extensional isomorphism, then our two
statements may be replaced by

(16) Under the correct system in question, every point has cor-
     related with it a combination of a vertical and a horizontal
     line.
(17) Under the (another) correct system in question, no point has
     correlated with it a combination of any other elements;

and these are entirely compatible with each other. They say
nothing about what makes up a point; each speaks only about
what makes up whatever is correlated with a point in the
correct system in question. Furthermore, since isomorphism
neither guarantees nor precludes identity (though guaranteed by
it), (16) makes no commitment, positive or negative, concerning

anything but lines and combinations of lines, while (17) makes none concerning anything but points. Thus these statements, which unlike (14) and (15) do not together claim that points are and are not made up of lines, may both be true in a world containing both lines and points—and indeed only in such a world.

Obviously, just as in passing from (9) and (10) to (11) and (12), we have lost something in passing from (14) and (15) to (16) and (17). In both cases we have effected a reconciliation by dispensing with the features responsible for the disagreement. There we abstracted from motion and contented ourselves with variations of distance with time; here we have abstracted from composition and contented ourselves with correlation. We have cancelled out the counterclaims of (14) and (15) and retreated to neutral statements.

And we may feel small loss. Whether a point is atomic or compound, and if compound what it comprises, depend heavily upon the basis and means of composition adopted for a system. Isn't this plainly, like frame of reference for motion, a matter of choice, while isomorphism of a correlation, like variation in distance with time, is a matter of fact? Most of us talk that way now and then, sometimes just before or just after decrying or denying the very distinction between convention and content. Which way shall we have it?

In any case, if the composition of points out of lines or of lines out of points is conventional rather than factual, points and lines themselves are no less so. Statements like (16) and (17) are not only neutral as to what makes up points or lines or regions but also neutral as to what these are. If we say that our sample space is a combination of points, or of lines, or of regions, or a combination of combinations of points, or lines, or regions, or a combination of all these together, or is a single lump, then since none of these is identical with any of the rest, we are giving one among countless alternative conflicting descriptions of what the space is. And so we may regard the disagreements as not about the facts but as due to differences in the conventions—of lines, points, regions, and modes of combination—adopted in organizing or describing the space. What, then, is the neutral fact or thing described in these different terms? Neither the space as (a) an undivided whole nor (b) as a combination of everything involved in the several accounts; for (a) and (b) are but two among the various ways of organizing it. But what is *it* that is so organized? When we strip off as layers of convention all differences among ways of describing *it*, what is left? The onion is peeled down to its empty core.

When we widen our purview to take in not just our sample space but all of space and everything else, the variety of contrasting versions multiplies enormously, and further reconciliations are sought by like means. Look back at our familiar example of apparent motion:

(18) A spot moves across the screen
(19) No spot so moves.

If we suppose that the realms of stimuli and of vision are entirely separate, the statements can be reconciled by segregation, much as in the case of opposing color descriptions applied to different parts of an object. But if, as is more usual, we regard the stimulus version and the visual version that these statements respectively belong to as covering the same territory in different ways, as different reports on a common world, then both the seen spot and the unseen stimuli will be missing from that common world. Again, statement (13) concerning variation in distance with time, although neutral relative to the opposing descriptions of the earth's motion in (9) and (10), is at odds with perceptual versions that admit no such physical objects as the earth. Physical objects and events and perceptual phenomena go the way of points and lines and regions and space.

In short, if we abstract from all features responsible for disagreements between truths we have nothing left but versions without things or facts or worlds. As Heraclitus or Hegel might have said, worlds seem to depend upon conflict for their existence. On the other hand, if we accept any two truths as disagreeing on the facts, and thus as true in different worlds, the grounds are not clear for discounting other conflicts between truths as mere differences in manner of speaking. To say for example that conflicting statements apply to the same world just insofar as they are about the same things would, reasonably, make (9) and (10) statements about the same world but would help very little in most cases. Do (14) and (15), for instance, speak of the same points? Is the screen that a dot moves across the same as the one no dot moves across? Is the seen table the same as the mess of molecules? To such questions, discussed at length in the philosophical literature, I suspect that the answer is a firm *yes* and a firm *no*. The realist will resist the conclusion that there is no world; the idealist will resist the conclusion that all conflicting versions describe different worlds. As for me, I find these views equally delightful and equally deplorable—for after all, the difference between them is purely conventional!

In practice, of course, we draw the line wherever we like, and change it as often as suits our purposes. On the level of theory, we flit back and forth between extremes as blithely as a physicist between particle and field theories. When the verbiage view threatens to dissolve everything into nothing, we insist that all true versions describe worlds. When the right-to-life sentiment threatens an overpopulation of worlds, we call it all talk. Or to put it another way, the philosopher like the philanderer is always finding himself stuck with none or too many.

Incidentally, recognition of multiple worlds or true versions suggests innocuous interpretations of necessity and possibility. A statement is necessary in a universe of worlds or true versions if true in all, necessarily false if true in none, and contingent or possible if true in some. Iteration would be construed in terms of universes of universes: a statement is necessarily necessary in such a superuniverse if necessarily true in all the member universes, etc. Analogues of theorems of a modal calculus follow readily. But such an account will hardly satisfy an avid advocate of possible worlds any more than spring water will satisfy an alcoholic.

## 3. Tests and Truth

Our foregoing conclusions or observations or suspicions bear upon the treatment of truth in at least three ways: A standard though uninformative formula concerning truth requires modification to a no more informative one; considerations other than truth take on added importance in the choice among statements or versions; and a hard problem concerning the relation between truth and tests for it may be slightly softened.

First, and of least importance, the familiar dictum " 'Snow is white' is true if and only if snow is white" must be revised to something like " 'Snow is white' is true in a given world if and only if snow is white in that world", which in turn, if differences between true versions cannot be firmly distinguished from differences between worlds, amounts merely to " 'Snow is white' is true according to a true version if and only if snow is white according to that version."

Second, that truths conflict reminds us effectively that truth cannot be the only consideration in choosing among statements or versions. As we have observed earlier, even where there is no conflict, truth is far from sufficient. Some truths are trivial, irrelevant, unintelligible, or redundant; too broad, too narrow, too boring, too bizarre, too complicated; or taken from some other version than the one in question, as when a guard, ordered to shoot any of his captives who moved, immediately shot them all and explained that they were moving rapidly around the earth's axis and around the sun.

Furthermore, we no more characteristically proceed by selecting certain statements as true and then applying other criteria to choose among them than by selecting certain statements as relevant and serviceable and then considering which among them are true. Rather we begin by excluding statements initially regarded as either false though perhaps otherwise right, or wrong though perhaps true, and go on from there. This account does not deny that truth is a necessary condition but deprives it of a certain preeminence.

But, of course, truth is no more a necessary than a sufficient consideration for a choice of a statement. Not only may the choice often be of a statement that is the more nearly right in other respects over one that is the more nearly true, but where truth is too finicky, too uneven, or does not fit comfortably with other principles, we may choose the nearest amenable and illuminating lie. Most scientific laws are of this sort: not assiduous reports of detailed data but sweeping Procrustean simplifications.

So irreverent a view of scientific laws is often resisted on the ground that they are implicitly only statements of approximation—that the " = " in "$v = p \cdot t$", for example, is to be read not as "equals" but as "approximately equals". Thus the sanctity and preeminence of truth is preserved. But whether we say that such a law is an approximation to truth or a true approximation matters very little. What does matter is that the approximations are preferred to what may be regarded either as truths or as more exact truths.

So far, I have been taking other criteria of rightness as supplementary to truth, and even at times contending with it. But do some of these other considerations serve also, or even rather, as tests for truth? After all, we must use some tests in judging truths; and such features as utility and coherence are prominent candidates. That we can readily produce ostensible examples of useless tangled truths and of useful neat falsehoods shows at most only that the tests are corroborative rather than conclusive. And good tests need not be conclusive; attraction by a magnet is a good but not conclusive test for iron. Nor need we be able to explain why utility or coherence or some other feature is any indication of truth. We may use the attraction as a test for iron without understanding at all the connection between the attraction and the composition of iron; all we need is to be satisfied that there is a reasonably reliable correlation between the two. And if the attraction is adopted as a test before we know the composition of iron, the correlation in question is between the attraction and either the results of other tests or a prior classification of objects as iron and not iron. Much the same may be said for truth; in the absence of any definitive and informative characterization, we apply various tests that we check against each other and against a rough and partial antecedent classification of statements as true and false. Truth, like intelligence, is perhaps just what the tests test; and the best account of what truth is may be an 'operational' one in terms of tests and procedures used in judging it.

Philosophers would like, though, to arrive at a characterization of truth as definitive as the scientific definition of iron; and some have argued with considerable ingenuity for the identification of truth with one or another accessible feature.

Notable among such efforts is the pragmatists' proposed interpretation of truth in terms of utility.[11] The thesis that true state-

---

[11] Nothing in this or the immediately following paragraphs is meant as a summary or caricature or defense or cavalier dismissal of any of the views discussed but only as a reminder of some of the problems and possibilities involved.

ments are those that enable us to predict or manage or defeat nature has no little appeal; but some conspicuous discrepancies between utility and truth have to be explained away. That utility unlike truth is a matter of degree can perhaps be dealt with by taking utility as measuring nearness to truth rather than as a criterion of truth itself. That utility unlike truth is relative to purpose might seem less serious when truth is recognized, as in the preceding pages, to be relative rather than absolute. But relativity to purpose does not align in any obvious way with relativity to world or version; for among alternative true versions or statements, some may be highly useful for many purposes, others for almost none and indeed much less useful than some falsehoods. Here a master argument will perhaps be put forth: that utility for one primary purpose—the acquisition of knowledge—can be identified with truth. But then the pragmatic thesis would seem to expire as it triumphs; that truths best satisfy the purpose of acquiring truths is as empty as evident.

Attempts to construe truth in terms of confident belief, or of credibility as some codification of belief—in terms of initial credibility together with inference, confirmation, probability, etc.[12] —face the obvious objection that the most credible statements often turn out to be false and the least credible ones true. Credibility thus seems no measure even of nearness to truth. But this obstacle may not be insurmountable. Consider for a moment the notion of permanence—taken here to mean lasting forever after some given time. Although we can never

---

[12] Credibility, though not identical with confidence, is here taken to be explicated in terms of it. We may be rather unsure of some statements that are highly confirmed, and stubbornly sure of others that are ill-confirmed; but confirmation and probability are the results of efforts to codify—and establish standards for—belief. See further "Sense and Certainty", *PP*, pp. 60–68; also *FFF*, pp. 62–65.

establish permanence of an object or material, we can establish durability in varying degrees short of permanence. Likewise, although we can never establish total and permanent credibility, we can establish strength and durability of credibility in varying degrees short of that. Shall we then identify unattainable total and permanent credibility with unattainable truth? To the ready protest that we might have total and permanent belief in a falsehood—that what is totally and permanently credible might not be true—perhaps the answer is that so long as the belief or credibility is indeed total and permanent, any divergence from the truth could never matter to us at all. Then if there is any such divergence, so much the worse for truth: scrap it in favor of total and permanent credibility. But, as Hartry Field has pointed out to me, total and permanent credibility can hardly be taken as a necessary condition for truth since a disjunction may be permanently and totally credible even though none of its components is.[13]

More venerable than either utility or credibility as definitive of truth is coherence, interpreted in various ways but always requiring consistency. The problems here, too, have been enormous. But the classic and chilling objection that for any coherent world version there are equally coherent conflicting versions weakens when we are prepared to accept some two conflicting versions as both true. And the difficulty of establishing any correlation between internal coherence and external correspondence diminishes when the very distinction between

---

[13]Compare C. S. Peirce's "Fixation of Belief" in *Collected Papers of Charles Sanders Peirce* (Cambridge, Mass., 1931-1958), Vol. V, pp. 223-247; but see Israel Scheffler's discussion of that paper in his *Four Pragmatists* (London, 1974), pp. 60-75.

*Note added in fifth printing:* In the present text, the end of the first paragraph has been revised, as have the last two sentences of the first full paragraph on page 139. The discussion of truth and acceptability here has been replaced by a drastically different treatment in *Reconceptions* by Nelson Goodman and Catherine Z. Elgin (Hackett, 1988) Chapter X.

the 'internal' and the 'external' is in question. As the distinction between convention and content—between what is said and how it is said—wilts, correspondence between version and world loses its independence from such features of versions as coherence. Of course coherence, however defined, rather than being sufficient for truth seems to operate conjointly with judgments of initial credibility in our efforts to determine truth.[14] But at least—and this is the third of the points mentioned at the beginning of the section—coherence and other so-called internal features of versions are no longer disqualified as tests for truth.

So much for this rather roller-coaster view of truth in relation to its companions and competitors. Now let us look at some clear cases where we judge with considerable confidence and constancy the rightness of what is neither true nor false.

## 4. Veracity and Validity

Among the most explicit and clearcut standards of rightness we have anywhere are those for validity of a deductive argument; and validity is of course distinct from truth in that the premises and conclusions of a valid argument may be false. Validity consists of conformity with rules of inference—rules that codify deductive practice in accepting or rejecting particular inferences.[15] Yet deductive validity, though different from is not altogether independent of truth, but so relates statements that valid inference from true premises gives true conclusions. Indeed, the primary function of valid inference is to relate truths to truths. Furthermore, validity is not the only requirement

---

[14] See *PP*, pp. 60–68.

[15] On this and other matters to be discussed in this section, see further *FFF*: III and IV. Incidentally, although validity is above identified with conformity to rules of inference, it is sometimes even in my own writings identified rather with overall rightness, which includes satisfaction of other requirements as well.

upon a right deductive argument. A deductive argument is right in a fuller sense only if the premisses are true and the inferences valid. Thus rightness of deductive argument, while involving validity, is still closely allied with truth.

Now consider inductive validity. Here again, neither truth of premisses nor truth of conclusion is required; and inductive like deductive validity consists of conformity with principles that codify practice. But inductive validity is one step further removed from truth than is deductive validity; for valid inductive inference from true premisses need not yield a true conclusion.

On the other hand, while inductive *rightness* like deductive rightness does require truth of the premisses as well as validity, it also requires something more.[16] To begin with, a right inductive argument must be based not only on true premisses but upon all the available genuine evidence. An inductive argument from positive instances of a hypothesis is not right if negative instances are omitted; all the examined instances must be taken into account. No parallel requirement is imposed upon a deductive argument, which is right if it proceeds validly from any true premisses, however incomplete.

Still, inductive rightness is not fully characterized as inductive validity plus use of all examined instances. If all examined instances have been examined before 1977, the argument that all instances whatever will be examined before 1977 is still inductively wrong; and even if all examined emeralds have been grue, still inductive argument to the hypothesis that all emeralds are grue is wrong. Inductive rightness requires evidence statements and the hypothesis to be in terms of 'genuine' or 'natural'

---

[16] A singular statement derived by instantiation from a hypothesis is a positive instance when determined by examination to be true, a negative instance when so determined to be false.

kinds—or in my terminology, to be in terms of projectible predicates like "green" and "blue" rather than in terms of nonprojectible predicates like "grue" and "bleen". Without such a restriction, right inductive arguments could always be found to yield countless conflicting conclusions: that all emeralds are green, are grue, are gred, etc.

In sum, then, inductive rightness requires that the argument proceed from premises consisting of all such true reports on examined instances as are in terms of projectible predicates. Thus inductive rightness, while still demanding truth of premises, makes severe additional demands. And although we hope by means of inductive argument to arrive at truth, inductive rightness unlike deductive rightness does not guarantee truth. A deductive argument is wrong and its inferences invalid if it reaches a false conclusion from true premises, but an inductive argument that is valid and right in all respects may yet reach a false conclusion from true premises. This vital difference has inspired some frantic and futile attempts to justify induction in the sense of showing that right induction will always, or more often than not, yield true conclusions. Any feasible justification of induction must consist rather of showing that the rules of inference codify inductive practice—that is, of effecting a mutual adjustment between rules and practice—and of distinguishing projectible predicates or inductively right categories from others.

This brings us, then, to the question what are inductively right categories, and so to a third kind of rightness in general: rightness of categorization. Such rightness is one step further removed from truth; for while deductive and inductive rightness still have to do with statements, which have truth-value, rightness of categorization attaches to categories or predicates—or systems thereof—which have no truth-value.

On the question what distinguishes right inductive categories from others, I can only indicate the nature of a tentative reply I have outlined elsewhere (*FFF*: IV). A primary factor in projectibility is habit; where otherwise equally well-qualified hypotheses conflict, the decision normally goes to the one with the better entrenched predicates. Obviously there must be leeway for progress, for the introduction of novel organizations that make, or take account of, newly important connections and distinctions. Inertia is modified by inquiry and invention, somewhat restrained in turn by entrenched general 'background' principles or metaprinciples, and so on.[17] The formulation of rules, based on these factors, that in effect define projectibility or right inductive categorization is a difficult and intricate task. Categories that are inductively right tend to coincide with categories that are right for science in general; but variations in purpose may result in variations in relevant kinds.

Sometimes the choice among versions adopting different categorizations, like the choice among descriptions of motion adopting different frames of reference, may be mainly for convenience. After all, we can somewhat awkwardly restate our ordinary inductive arguments in terms like "grue" and "bleen" much as we can translate a heliocentric into a geocentric system. We need only replace "green" by "grue if examined before *t* and otherwise bleen" and replace "blue" by "bleen if examined before *t* and otherwise grue". Nevertheless, according to present practice, the blue-green categorization is right and the grue-bleen categorization wrong as marking the lines along which we make our inductive inferences. The penalty for using wrong

---

[17] See *FFF*, p. 97; also "On Kahane's Confusions", *Journal of Philosophy*, Vol. 69 (1972), pp. 83–84, and my comments on Kutschera's paper, *Erkenntnis*, Vol. 12 (1978), pp. 282–284.

categories is not merely an inconvenience any more than the result of the guard's choice of a wrong frame of reference was merely an inconvenience to the slaughtered captives. "Shoot if they change in color" could have been equally fatal if the guard were projecting abnormal color predicates. Induction according to nonprojectible categories is not merely awkward but wrong, whatever may be the outcome of the inductive conclusion drawn. Rightness of induction requires rightness of predicates projected, and that in turn may vary with practice.

Every so often a critic of one of my writings complains that on some topic I 'state without argument that...'. A particular example I vaguely remember from somewhere reads something like: "Goodman states without argument that the core of representation is denotation." This led me to reflect on why I made so crucial a declaration without argument. And the reason is that argument in any sense that involves inference from premises would be utterly inappropriate here. In such a context, I am not so much stating a belief or advancing a thesis or a doctrine as proposing a categorization or scheme of organization, calling attention to a way of setting our nets to capture what may be significant likenesses and differences. Argument for the categorization, the scheme, suggested could not be for its truth, since it has no truth-value, but for its efficacy in worldmaking and understanding. An argument would consist rather of calling attention to important parallels between pictorial representation and verbal denotation, of pointing out obscurities and confusions that are clarified by this association, of showing how this organization works with other aspects of the theory of symbols. For a categorial system, what needs to be shown is not that it is true but what it can do. Put crassly, what is called for in such cases is less like arguing than selling.

## 5. Right Representation

Validity of deductive and inductive inference and projectibility of predicates are in varying degrees independent of truth, but not of language. All are standards applicable to versions in words. What about rightness of nonverbal versions? When, for example, is a pictorial representation correct?

Two familiar answers are that a representation is right to the extent that it resembles what it depicts, and that a representation is right if in effect it makes a true statement. Neither answer is satisfactory.

The shortcomings of the first answer, in terms of resemblance, have been so fully set forth in the literature[18] as to make any detailed discussion here superfluous. Correctness of representation like correctness of description varies with system or framework; the question "Is the picture correct?" is in this way like the question "Does the earth move?" A picture drawn in reversed or otherwise distorted perspective,[19] or replacing colors by their complementaries, can be as correct under the given system as a picture we call realistic under the current standard Western system of representation. But here we must remember that there are two different uses of "realistic". According to the more frequent usage, a picture is realistic to the extent that it is correct under the accustomed system of representation; for example, in the present Western culture, a picture by Dürer is more realistic than a picture by Cézanne. Realistic or right representation in this sense, like right categorization, requires observance of custom and tends to correlate loosely with ordinary judgments of resemblance, which likewise rest upon habit.

---

[18] E.g., in E. H. Gombrich, *Art and Illusion* (New York, 1960), various passages, and in *LA*: I.

[19] See my note "On J. J. Gibson's New Perspective", *Leonardo*, Vol. 4 (1971), pp. 359–360.

On the other hand, a representation unrealistic by this standard may picture quite correctly under a different system, much as the earth may dance the role of Petrouchka under a certain unusual frame of reference. And an 'unnatural' frame or system may be right in some circumstances through prevailing in another culture or winning adoption for special purposes. When a painter or photographer makes, or discloses to us, erstwhile unseen aspects of a world, he is sometimes said to have achieved a new degree of realism by discovering and presenting new aspects of reality. What we have here, in representation under a right system strange to us, is realism in the sense not of habituation but of revelation. The two senses of "realistic" reflect the factors of inertia and initiative we saw contending in the case of rightness of induction and categorization.

The trouble with the other answer to the question of rightness of representation—the answer in terms of the truth of a statement supposedly made by a picture—is that a picture makes no statement. The picture of a huge yellow wrecked antique car, like the description "the huge yellow wrecked antique car", does not commit itself to any of the following statements:

The huge yellow wrecked car is antique
The huge yellow antique car is wrecked
The huge wrecked antique car is yellow
The yellow wrecked antique car is huge,

or to any other. Although representations and descriptions differ in important ways, in neither case can correctness be a matter of truth.

For descriptive as well as for declarative versions, conflict can be construed in terms of negation: "always red everywhere" and "never red anywhere" conflict, while "green" and "round" do not. And where two right versions conflict and cannot be reconciled in some such way as illustrated earlier, they are of different worlds if any. But for representational versions, where there is no explicit negation, what distinguishes between a pair of right pictures of different things and a pair of different right pictures of the same thing? Do a Soutine painting and a Utrillo drawing, the one in thick impasto and curved lines showing a facade with two twisted windows, the other in straight black lines showing a facade with a door and five windows, represent different buildings or the same building in different ways? We must bear in mind here that even for declarative versions we could draw no clear and firm general distinction between the matter and the manner of discourse. Sometimes a sentence and its negate are reconcilable in one way or another—for example, as applying to different parts or periods of a world. Likewise two moving pictures, one of a sphere rotating clockwise and the other of a sphere rotating counterclockwise, may picture the earth equally correctly from different points of view. Showing that two versions are of the same world involves showing how they fit together. And the question about the Soutine and the Utrillo is much like the question whether a certain mess of molecules and my table are the same.

Such matters aside, a statement is true, and a description or representation right, for a world it fits. And a fictional version, verbal or pictorial, may if metaphorically construed fit and be right for a world. Rather than attempting to subsume descriptive and representational rightness under truth, we shall do better, I think, to subsume truth along with these under the general notion of rightness of fit.[20] That brings us, before we examine

---

[20] Readers of foregoing pages will be well aware that none of this implies either that any ready-made world lies waiting to be described or represented, or that wrong as well as right versions make worlds they fit. See further Section 7 below.

further the nature and criteria of right fit, to versions that are neither factual nor fictional statements, descriptions, or representations.

## 6. The Fair Sample

Rightness of abstract visual or musical works will have such aspects as rightness of design, and here we risk an accusation of invading the sacrosanct realm of beauty rather than keeping to kinds of rightness at all comparable to truth. Any such protest would betray an attitude antithetical to my insistence on the very continuity and unity, the very affinity, of art and science and perception as branches of worldmaking. Rightness of abstract works, or of nondenotational aspects of nonabstract works, is neither identical with nor utterly alien to truth; both are species of a more general notion of rightness. To say that beauty or aesthetic rightness is truth or that it is incomparable with truth seem to me equally misleading slogans, and I mention beauty here only to exclude it from further consideration.

We saw earlier that works or other symbols that do not declare or describe or represent anything, literally or metaphorically, or even purport to denote anything, may present worlds by exemplification. What constitutes rightness or wrongness of such exemplification? When is a sample right?

Most obviously, just as a predicate or other label may be wrongly applied to a given object—as say, "red" to a green object—so an object may be a wrong sample in that it is not even an instance of the label, does not possess the property in question. But also, something may be an instance of a predicate or property without being a sample of it, as in the case of the tailor's swatch that is an instance of a certain size and shape but not, since it does not refer to these features, a sample of them.

A further question, therefore, is whether what actually is a sample of a feature[21] may still not be a right sample of it. We have noticed that even though all examined emeralds are grue, inductive argument to "All emeralds are grue" is wrong, and that even though the captives did move, the guard should not have shot them. But this, while it may offer some hints toward an approach to our present question, suggests no immediate answer.

In common parlance, we do distinguish between not being a sample of a feature and being a sample but not a fair sample. A swatch cut from a bolt and used as a sample is not always a fair sample. It may be too small to show the pattern at all or else so cut as to show a component motif only partially or in a misleading orientation. The five samples sketched in Figure 5 may all have come from the same bolt. Each contains the same amount of material as the rest, and of course none contains the whole pattern, which may consist of many long bands.[22]. Yet among

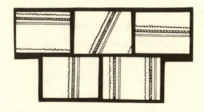

**Figure 5**

---

[21] Since "property" is customarily so closely associated with "predicate", I often use the term "feature" in the hope that it may come to serve as a reminder that not all labels are verbal.

[22] Patterns exemplified may vary greatly in specificity, as *e.g.*, striped, pin-striped, blue and white quarter-inch pin-striped, etc. Exemplification like denotation may thus be more or less general; but whereas generality of a predicate is a matter of scope of application, generality of a sample is a matter of scope of exemplified feature.

the five, the one at the lower right may be the only fair sample. Why is this so? What does it mean?

Before we try to answer, let us look at the somewhat different case of samples of the grass seed mixture in a given barrel. On occasion, we may apply either of two criteria for being a fair sample of the mixture: first, that the mixture in the sample is in the same proportion as in the barrel; or second, that the sample has been fairly drawn in that the contents of the barrel have been thoroughly stirred, parts of the sample taken without prejudice from various levels, etc. Although the rationale for the first criterion is clear, such criteria are inapplicable in many cases and we resort to much less easily defended criteria like the second. When we know the proportion of the various kinds of seed in the barrel, we can make a sample fair in the first sense by keeping the proportions in the sample the same. But when we take samples of sea water or drinking water, we cannot know—though we hope—that the samples are fair in the first sense; we rely upon what we consider to be fairness in taking the samples as a basis for supposing that the samples accurately reflect the mixture in the harbor or reservoir. But what determines such fairness in sampling?

The question—and the answer—should have a familiar ring. A sample fair in this sense is one that may be rightly projected to the pattern or mixture or other relevant feature of the whole or of further samples. Such fairness or projectibility, rather than requiring or guaranteeing agreement between the projection made and an actual feature of the whole or of further samples, depends upon conformity to good practice in interpreting samples—that is, both in proceeding from sample to feature in question[23] and in determining whether that feature is

---

[23] Requirements upon procedure will vary with need in different cases: for the seed samples, the proportion of types of seed must be selected rather than such other features as the actual count; for the tailor's swatch, the pattern in question might be constructed by a standard juxtaposition of iterations of the patch.

projectible. Good practice, in turn, depends upon habit in continual revision under frustration and invention. When the out-
comes of rightly made predictions are wrong, the failures may
be blamed on bad luck or, if they are prominent or plentiful,
may call for amendment of what constitutes good practice.
Some accord among samples is a test of good practice and of
fairness of sample; but also such accord depends heavily upon
what labels or kinds are relevant and right. Thus here as well as
in ordinary induction entrenchment-novelty is a major factor,
entering into the determination of what is exemplified, of
whether the sample is fairly taken, of whether the exemplified
feature is projectible, and of what constitutes accord among
samples. Indeed, projectibility from evidence differs from fairness of sample primarily in that while evidence and hypotheses
are statements, samples and what they exemplify may be nonlinguistic. Thus some samples and the nonverbal labels or features exemplified by or projectible from them may, unlike evidence statements and hypotheses, belong to symbol systems
that are neither denotational nor articulate.[24]

Although in the case of the cloth and the seed, I have usually
been speaking as if the projection of pattern or mixture were to
the whole bolt or barrel or reservoir, we more typically project
rather to other fairly taken portions: to packages of seed, or suit-
lengths of cloth, or drinks of water. And this is worth noting for
several reasons. First, such portions, which are often of primary
interest to us, may all be quite different from the whole in the
required respect; for instance, even if the barrel mix is 50–50,

---

[24] On articulate or finitely differentiated as contrasted with dense symbol systems, see *LA*: IV.

each package might contain seed all of one kind or the other. Second, accord among samples, not satisfied in such an event, is thus a more direct test of fairness of sample for normal projection. And third, our attention is called to the sort of accord called for among samples: the swatches need not all be the same so long as the same pattern results from them by appropriate construction; and the packages of seed need not all have exactly the same mixture, say 50–50, but only need center around this ratio in a preferred statistical way (as median, mean, or mode) or just in that the logical sum of all the samples taken has approximately the 50–50 mix.

Works of art are not specimens from bolts or barrels but samples from the sea. They literally or metaphorically exemplify forms, feelings, affinities, contrasts, to be sought in or built into a world. The features of the whole are undetermined; and fairness of sample is no matter of shaking a barrel thoroughly or taking water from scattered places but rather of coordination of samples. In other words, rightness of design, color, harmonics— fairness of a work as a sample of such features—is tested by our success in discovering and applying what is exemplified. What counts as success in achieving accord depends upon what our habits, progressively modified in the face of new encounters and new proposals, adopt as projectible kinds. A Mondrian design is right if projectible to a pattern effective in seeing a world. When Degas painted a woman seated near the edge of the picture and looking out of it, he defied traditional standards of composition but offered by example a new way of seeing, of organizing experience. Rightness of design differs from rightness of representation or description not so much in nature or standards as in the type of symbolization and mode of reference involved.

## 7. Rightness Reviewed

Briefly, then, truth of statements and rightness of descriptions, representations, exemplifications, expressions—of design, drawing, diction, rhythm—is primarily a matter of fit: fit to what is referred to in one way or another, or to other renderings, or to modes and manners of organization. The differences between fitting a version to a world, a world to a version, and a version together or to other versions fade when the role of versions in making the worlds they fit is recognized. And knowing or understanding is seen as ranging beyond the acquiring of true beliefs to the discovering and devising of fit of all sorts.

Procedures and tests used in the search for right versions range from deductive and inductive inference through fair sampling and accord among samples. Despite our faith in such tests, their claims as means for determining rightness may often seem obscure. Indeed, rather than being able to justify our confidence in inductive inference or in the procedures for taking fair samples, we look to the confidence itself for whatever justification there may be for these procedures. Choosing "green" rather than "grue" as projectible, or stirring and shaking a barrel of seed, may seem like rain-dancing—ritual with some celebrated successes and some dismissed failures that is cherished until too disastrous or disreputable. But so sour a view betrays a discredited demand for justification as convincing argument that a test or procedure will ensure, or at least improve our chances of, reaching right conclusions. We have seen, on the contrary, that rightness of categorization, which enters into most other varieties of rightness, is rather a matter of fit with practice; that without the organization, the selection of relevant kinds, effected by evolving tradition, there is no rightness or wrongness of categorization, no validity or invalidity of inductive inference, no fair or unfair sampling, and no uniformity or disparity among samples. Thus justifying such tests for rightness may consist primarily in showing not that they are reliable but that they are authoritative.

All the same, tests results are transient while we think of truth and rightness as eternal. The passing of many and varied tests increases acceptability; but what is once maximally acceptable may later be unacceptable. Total and permanent acceptability, though, may be taken as a sufficient condition of rightness. Such ultimate acceptability, while as inaccessible as absolute rightness, is nevertheless explicable in terms of the tests and their results.

Whether a picture is rightly designed or a statement correctly describes is tested by examination and reexamination of the picture or statement and what it refers to in one way or another, by trying its fit in varied applications and with other patterns and statements. One thinks again of Constable's intriguing remark, stressed by Gombrich,[25] that painting is a science of which pictures are the experiments. Agreement on or among initial untested judgments,[26] and their survival upon testing, is rather rare for either designs or statements. Furthermore, rightness of design and truth of statement are alike relative to system: a design that is wrong in Raphael's world may be right in Seurat's, much as a description of the stewardess's motion that is wrong from the control tower may be right from the passenger's seat; and such relativity should not be mistaken for subjectivity in either case. The vaunted claim of community of

---

[25] *Art and Illusion*, p. 33 and elsewhere.

[26] "Judgment" as used here must be freed of exclusive association with statements; it includes, for example, apprehension of the fit of a design, and the decisions a pool-player takes in aiming his shots.

opinion among scientists is mocked by fundamental controversies raging in almost every science from psychology to astrophysics. And judgments of the Parthenon and the Book of Kells have hardly been more variable than judgments of the laws of gravitation.[27] I am not claiming that rightness in the arts is less subjective, or even no more subjective, than truth in the sciences, but only suggesting that the line between artistic and scientific judgment does not coincide with the line between subjective and objective, and that any approach to universal accord on anything significant is exceptional.

My readers could weaken that latter conviction by agreeing unanimously with the foregoing somewhat tortuous and in a double sense trying course of thought.

---

[27] Curiously, such observations are sometimes adduced to show that since science progresses while art does not, judgments of scientific truth are more objective than judgments of artistic rightness. The reason that earlier theories but not older works may be rendered obsolete by later ones is often, I think, that the earlier theories, insofar as sound, are absorbed into and are rederivable from the later while works of art, functioning differently as symbols, cannot be absorbed into or derived from others. I cannot here go into the details of this explanation.

# NAME INDEX

Allen, Woody, 96, 96n, 101
Anaximander, 97–99
Anscombe, G. E. M., 10n

Bally, C., 27n
Beardsley, Monroe, 49n, 102n
Beck, J., 82n
Bruner, Jerome S., 6, 6n, 14n, 16n

Carnap, Rudolf, 114n
Cassirer, Ernst, 1–2, 4, 5, 6, 14n
Church, Alonzo, 53, 53n
Clark, Kenneth, 32n

Democritus, 98, 99

Elsner, Ann, 82n
Empedocles, 98–9
Exner, Sigmund, 72

Fecht, W., 81n
Field, Hartry, 124

Gardner, Howard, 24n
Gibson, J. J., 80, 130n
Gombrich, E. H., 6, 6n, 14, 14n, 23n, 130n, 139
Goodman, Nelson, 19n, 24n, 129
Grüsser, O.-J., 81n
Grüsser-Cornehls, Ursula, 81n

Hanson, Norwood, 96–7
Henle, M., 87n
Heraclitus, 98, 119
Hernadi, Paul, 67n
Hirsch, E. D., Jr., 24, 24n
Hough, Graham, 24, 24n, 27n
Howard, Vernon, ix, 24n, 50n, 52n

James, William, 2

Kahane, Howard, 128n
Kanizsa, Gaetano, 87n
Kant, Immanuel, x
Kennedy, John, 87n
Kolers, Paul, ix, 15n, 16, 72–9, 76n, 80–84, 82n, 88, 92
Kutschera, F. v., 128n

Land, Edwin H., 89n
Langer, Susanne, 1n
Lettvin, Jerome Y., 73n, 81n
Lewis, C. I., x
Llinas, R., 81n
Lynch, Kevin, 13n

Maturana, H. K., 73n
McCarthy, Mary, 57–8, 57n
McCulloch, W. S., 73n

Nagel, Alan, 67n

Parmenides, 98–9
Peirce, Charles S., 22n, 124n
Perkins, David, 24n
Pitts, W. H., 73n
Polanyi, M., 22n
Pollaiuolo, Antonio, 28–9, 31
Putnam, Hilary, ix

Quine, W. V. O., ix, 114n

Rock, I., 89n
Roelots, C. O., 73
Rorty, Richard, 4n
Rudner, R., 104n

141

# SUBJECT INDEX